A Winner in Spite of . . .

A Winner in Spite of...

Evelyn Smith Booker

A Winner in Spite of . . .

Printed in the United States of America
ISBN 978-1-946425-79-9 softcover
ISBN 978-1-946425-80-5 hardcover

Book Design by CSinclaire Write-Design
Cover Design by Klevur

I dedicate this book to my parents,
Henry Roland and Eulah Belle Smith,
and my sisters and brothers who have
already joined the heavenly choir,
Leamon (Maggie)
Novella Adams (Charles),
Ruberta Vereen (Owen),
Henry Raymond Smith (Arvella),
Rufus Benjamin Smith (Dorothy),
and Archie Thurman Smith (Shirley).

To my husband, Lee Weldon Booker,
our daughters, Millicent Candene Booker Ford (Kenneth)
and Eulonda Lea Booker Pfister (Roger)

To our grandchildren,
KJ Ford, Mackenzie Blair Ford,
Nathan Grey Pfister, Ashlynn Nicole Pfister,
and Madelyn Eve Pfister

To my surviving siblings,
sisters Esther Morse (Decatur),
Ethel Powell (Joe), and Clara Vaun,
and brothers
Roy Latson (Helen),
Ervin, and Jerome (Rosa)

CONTENTS

Why I Wrote This Book

I had the opportunity to hear a dynamic, international motivational speaker years ago. He told a quick story of how he had been traveling overseas for a week and was looking forward to flying home and seeing his beautiful wife and two wonderful children. When he arrived, his family greeted him with hugs and kisses.

As soon as he got in the car, his wife immediately reminded him, "At noon today, you gotta take Anna for piano lessons, and at three, you gotta take John for baseball practice."

He said, "I reflected that 'I got to' sounds like an obligation. What if I rephrased this to '*I get to take* Anna to piano, and *I get to take* John for baseball practice.' That's an opportunity and all of the positives that come along with 'I get to.' And I have transportation, gas, money, children with talents, eyesight, activities of my limbs, and the list is endless."

To me that attitude changes everything. Think of the power of us changing our thinking from "I've got to" to "I get to." With that said, I "get to" share a few of my thoughts and experiences in life in this book. I am not really writing a memoir or a "self-help" book or a business "how to succeed" book. This is not a story of my life, either personal or corporate. You will, however, find a little about my growing up time, a smattering about my work years, a dab about my family, a lot about my faith, and a few doses of basic, down-to-earth, practical advice dropped in. I do share some of my achievements because many would consider them against the odds, and I review with you instances where Blacks, especially young Black men, have not won against the odds—and that needs to change. In other words, I "get to" share some here-and-there thoughts with you in the hope that maybe some good will come from them.

I hope what I share in the parts about my life will be an inspiration, a motivation, and an encouragement to many, regardless of age. No matter who you are or where you come from, there are no limits to who you can be or what you can accomplish. *As long as you seek God's guidance on His plan, you will find His purpose for you in this grand universe.* A winner never quits, and a quitter never wins. WE ARE ALL WINNERS if we choose to be.

Henry Ford is credited with saying "Whether you think you can, or think you can't—you're right." This is my long-held philosophy that I say just a little bit differently: If you think you can, or if you think you can't, you're right. I KNOW THAT I CAN, and I believe that you can too!

Growing Up

CHAPTER 1

I Have Been Made Ready

I am of a royal priesthood . . .
– 1 Peter 2:9

I am more than a conqueror . . .
– Romans 8:31-32

I can do all things through Christ who strengthens me . . .
– Philippians 4:13

I speak things that are not, as though they are, in order for them to be . . .
– Romans 4:17

As I contemplated the possibility of writing a book, so many thoughts came to mind in reference to subjects, topics to include, occurrences not to include, and a broad spectrum of emotions. I concluded that I should just begin and so I did.

Once I retired on March 11, 2011 from Capitol Broadcasting after thirty years, I filled my life with many things. Now, my inner spirit says there is no time like the present to write this book. We each have our own journey. This is a glimpse of mine.

~

To start, I have to say that retirement is such an incredible phase in life, a marvelous milestone to reach. Retirement affords you so many wonderful opportunities for memory-making moments that you cannot put a price tag on. It has allowed my husband, Lee, and me time for visiting our older two grands for Grandparent's Day in Arkansas. We even received the award for traveling the farthest one year! We've been able to celebrate special occasions such as Thanksgiving, Christmas, and holidays with our Smith/Ford/Pfister/Booker families. Lee and I helped take care of our three youngest grands, and we were the daycare for Nathan (our youngest grand at the time) for 18 months. Nothing compares to quality family time.

Wonderful family time aside, I want to share one misadventure that ended in a very surprising way. I share this with you now at the beginning of this book because, to me, it perfectly tells of God's hand and His grace that have always been, and continue to be, present in my life.

~

On a cool, beautiful Friday afternoon, Lee was cooking fish and shrimp on the back deck as I was preparing the coleslaw, hush puppies, and cornbread inside. Our grandson Nathan was sitting in his high chair, peering out the window. All of a sudden, Nathan began screaming and pointing toward the window. The pot of hot oil had begun to spill over and catch fire while Lee had stepped inside for a moment. When Lee saw the pan was burning, he ran to it and grabbed it from the heat. The hot oil popped and started to burn his hands and face. I saw Lee's face and hands afire.

I immediately rushed to help him pull off his shirt while the pot was still burning.

As soon as I could, I called our daughter, Millicent, a doctor, and she answered on the first ring. I never call her at work. She said when she saw my number, she answered immediately because she knew that something had to be wrong. She instructed us not to wipe his face and to get to the ER as soon as possible.

When we got to the emergency room, we were told that Lee had third degree burns. Surprisingly, they did not instruct us to go to the hospital that evening. I took pictures of the burns and sent them to Millicent and to Cheri, our son-in-law Roger's sister, who works at UNC Hospital. Cheri got Lee scheduled for an appointment with the UNC Burn Center. Until then he was given meds and explicit care instructions. It was my responsibility to administer and apply medications and to change the dressings (wearing gloves) on his face and hands every four hours over the weekend. It seemed that his shirt had protected his chest.

When we sent the pictures of the burns, the doctors told us to prepare Lee to be hospitalized for at least a week as they would have to do skin grafts. However, when we arrived on Monday morning, the doctors and nurses examined him and handed him white wash cloths to wipe his face. All of the burned smut wiped off.

Lee and I had been using a particular skin care product for approximately a year prior to the burn incident. The doctors concluded that the product literally preserved his skin. They were shocked and amazed that there was no visible skin damage, however, they told us that the pigmentation in his face and hands would never return to normal.

We left the hospital with a two-week follow-up scheduled. Lee was told to wear a wide-brimmed hat that the hospital provided, sunscreen, and sunglasses "forever."

If you were to look at his face and hands today, you would not be able to tell that he was ever burned. SIMPLY MIRACULOUS. Thank God for the angels that were assigned to us at birth.

ALL THAT I AM, ALL THAT I HAVE, I OWE TO GOD'S LOVE, GRACE, MERCY, AND FAVOR!

Now come take this journey with me as I share the place, purpose, and plan designed for me.

CHAPTER 2

Choices

Trust in the Lord with all your heart and do not rely on your own insight. In all your ways acknowledge him, and he will make straight your paths.

– Proverbs 3:5 - 6

"CHOICE is the most important tool we have. Everything boils down to choice. We exist in a field of infinite possibilities. Every choice we make shuts an infinite number of doors and opens an infinite number of doors. At any point we change the directions of our lives by a simple choice. It is all in our hands, our hearts, our minds." — **Tinybuddha.com**

Everything that we do on a daily basis requires making a choice as our Master divinely orchestrates it all. As simple as it sounds, this is the foundation of everything for each of us: making the right choices.

Consider the routine choices as basic as starting your day. You have choices to make about getting up every morning, choosing whether to work remotely or to commute the distance. You have to decide what to eat and what to wear. Of course, with COVID-19 running rampant as I write this, some choices are different now!

However, a very important choice that you make daily is the attitude that you embrace for the day. That attitude will determine the day, good, bad, or indifferent, that you will have, so it behooves you to declare that it's going to be an OUTSTANDING day. Take a look in the mirror each morning and say with conviction, "Today is going to be an absolutely MARVELOUS day."

A reminder from SimpleReminders.com about choice says:

A person's most useful asset is not a head full of knowledge, but a heart full of love, an ear ready to listen and a hand willing to help others.

Make it a choice to embrace a healthy, positive attitude every day and share it with others. Say something to put a smile on someone's face, encourage somebody, and be thankful for how God has so richly blessed you.

From small, routine choices to life-altering, life-affirming choices, consider them all well. Doors close and doors open. Life moves a path forward based on your choices, little or big.

CHAPTER 3

Humble Beginnings

It's not what we have in life,
it's WHO we have in our lives that matters.
–J. M. Laurence

As I sat the night of September 14, 2018 listening to strong winds and rain beating on the windows, many thoughts entered my mind. Hurricane Florence was pounding the shores of North and South Carolina. What a night to begin penning the "Humble Beginnings" chapter of my book as I pulled my birth certificate from the file. It read:

Evelyn Faye Smith
DOB: 6/23/1951
Place of Birth: Columbus County, NC
Father: Henry Roland Smith (Age 37)
Mother: Eulah Belle Long Smith (Age 34)
Address: Route 3, Box 90, Nakina, NC
Other children now living: 7
Midwife: Mattie Chatman
Time of Birth: 1PM

My dad would always tell the story that many births happened the day I was born. The cow had a calf, a sow had a litter, a cat had kittens, and our dog Motley had puppies! It seemed like a wonderful start. However, three days after I was born, I fell into a deep sleep. I did no eating, drinking, or bodily elimination. Mom was still extremely weak from the delivery—I was born at home. My dad and my oldest sister, Esther, took me to a doctor in Whiteville. The doctor told them he had never encountered a baby this young not responding at all. He suggested that they keep rubbing my feet gently and, hopefully, I would wake up soon. Esther said my dad kept saying, "Don't let her go to sleep" and her reply was, "Daddy, all she's doing is sleeping!"

After three office visits and no positive response, Mom asked Daddy to call Rev. Dave Flowers, the pastor of our church, Zion Plain Baptist. It seemed I was the talk of the town. Rev. Flowers lived in Longwood, which was 20 miles from Nakina. Dad asked if he could come and pray for me. Rev. Flowers was known throughout North Carolina as a prophet with healing hands.

Rev. Flowers came and asked the family to form a circle and hold hands while he prayed. I have been told a portion of his prayer was this: "God, your word says, 'where two or three are touching and agreeing, and asking anything in your name, you will grant it' so now we are touching and agreeing, and we are asking in the name of Jesus that you touch this baby, wake her, bring her back to this family. We are thanking you in advance, we count it done, and we walk in victory."

Rev. Flowers told my parents and siblings that I would be awake by the time he reached Seven Creeks Church, which was at the end of our dirt road. That would be within three to five minutes.

As my family tells the account, when he was driving out

of our driveway, I opened my eyes, began stretching, screaming, nursing Mom, and everything started "moving"! OH WHAT A DAY!

The word spread rapidly that Rev. Flowers had come, laid hands on the infant, prayed, and there was another miracle. I was back!

As an avid Bible reader now, I know the passages that Rev. Flowers referenced were Matthew 18:19: "Again, truly I tell you, if two of you agree on earth about anything you ask, it will be done for you by my Father in heaven." and Matthew 7:7: "Ask, and it will be given you; search, and you will find; knock, and the door will be opened for you." and Matthew 21:22: "Whatever you ask for in prayer with faith, you will receive."

My sister Esther, who is now 83 years young, still tells this story and gets emotional. In fact, she shared it at my retirement celebration in March of 2011.

As of that moment, with that prayer and laying on of hands by Rev. Flowers and my parents' faith and trust in God, I was touched, predestined for a purpose, at six days old.

Being the eighth of ten children and reared in a small town in southeastern North Carolina, there was never a dull moment in the Smith house. Our mom was pregnant for much of 20 years, giving birth every two years. The pattern was two girls, Esther and Ethel, two boys, Henry and Rufus, two more boys, Archie and Roy, two girls, Clara and Evelyn, and last, two boys, Ervin and Jerome. Mom was such a strong, intelligent, beautiful, and most importantly, God-fearing woman. We also have three wonderful siblings, Leamon, Novella, and Ruberta from before Dad met, courted, and married Mom.

Growing up on a farm afforded us opportunities and benefits that other people don't have a chance to experience.

We had fresh milk from the cow, homemade butter for home cooked made-from-scratch biscuits, sausage and bacon from our pigs, and vegetables galore from our garden. As I close my eyes and my senses kick into high gear, I can smell and taste dinner now. We planted, gathered, and canned or froze what we grew, so that we had plenty to eat during the winter months until it was planting and harvesting season again.

Our garden produced string beans, butter beans, okra, and purple-hull peas plus collard greens that were then blanched, chilled, and frozen.

The sweet potatoes we grew were stored differently. Dad and the boys would build a potato bank shaped somewhat like an igloo, alternating a layer of straw followed by a layer of dirt until the bank stood about 4 feet tall. There was a door to enter, retrieve the potatoes, and exit. I can smell those sweet potatoes baking in the oven now. The aroma is so memorable and sweet.

In addition to farming, our dad worked for Georgia Pacific, still one of the world's largest pulp and paper companies. Our mom was a domestic engineer and was very active with our schools, volunteering, and keeping check on us. Our parents loved us all—unconditionally. There were certain expectations of us. Beds had to be crisply made daily before we left for school, work, or church. We had to select our clothes the night before, polish our shoes, and police the den and ditches prior to going to bed. The bathrooms had to be spotless. Responsibilities were distributed equally. We learned important values growing up that have stood up well for us our whole lives.

People talk about core values or personal values. What exactly does that mean? If you had to list your top five core values, what would you list? Your values are the things you feel are important in the way you live and work. If you were to interview my siblings and me, our top five would, in all probability, be very similar.

Our parents instilled in us the importance of working hard, being dependable, being loyal, and having drive, commitment, and dedication, but most important was the love for family. They were the perfect example of practicing the Golden Rule found in Matthew 7:12: "In everything do to others as you would have them do to you . . . " Treat others the way you'd like to be treated. That shouldn't be too hard or asking too much. Can you imagine if everyone practiced this what the world would be? A much better place in which to live!

Our Brooks family (first cousins), Vereen family (railroad neighbors), and Smith family (first cousins), who lived through the woods from Grandma Missy's house, were one big community. For entertainment, we would play softball or baseball for hours on Saturday and Sunday afternoons. These incredible families remain friends today. Friendships, relationships—it's a part of who we are.

The true roadmap that our parents taught us from an early age was the Ten Commandments. These can be found in Exodus 20:2–13 and Deuteronomy 5:6–17.

Both of our parents stressed the necessity of getting an education. They taught us that we are just as smart, if not smarter, than anyone else. The major difference is how we apply our God-given talents and smarts. Because of God's grace, mercy, and favor, my siblings and I have done exceptionally well, and we have all retired from corporate America. I know our parents are extremely proud and smiling from heaven, saying, "Well done!"

Do you believe in angels? Well I do, and there are 43 references to angels in the Bible, substantiating that we have angels watching over us. It should give us great comfort in believing that they are always with us, encamped around us, and delivering us as we read about in Psalm 34:7. I firmly believe that once our loved ones, our parents in particular, leave us, they serve as angels. I dream about Mom often and sporadically about Dad. When I am speaking, my mom typically perches on my right shoulder and whispers that I'm "going to do great!"

Old barn in Nakina, North Carolina

Tobacco field

Tobacco transplanter

Reeves Ferry where I was baptized

Dirt road leading to Reeves Ferry

CHAPTER 4

Elementary School Days

Learn from yesterday, live for today, hope for tomorrow. The important thing is not to stop questioning . . .
– Albert Einstein

September 5, 2019, was a gloomy overcast Thursday morning. Hurricane Dorian was raging, pushing rain bands across the Bahamas and now hitting the South Carolina and North Carolina shores. I listened to the network news, flipping back and forth to local coverage, about reports of tornado touchdowns from North Myrtle Beach to Surfside. This brought back so many memories as Hurricane Florence was creating devastation this same time period the previous year with almost the identical path. This touched my heart because this is my "neck of the woods," very close to where I was born and reared in Columbus County. Memories flooded my mind.

When I think back over my early childhood, I distinctly remember our elementary school days. Our dad was off to work at Georgia Pacific and our mom would rise early. As we were getting dressed for school, the aroma of homemade biscuits, sausage, scrambled eggs, and buttered grits filled the air. Our neighbors from "up the railroad," the Vereen family, and our first cousins, the Brooks family, always said nothing in the world compared to Aunt (Mrs.) Eulah Belle's grits. Very scrumptious!

The three families would wait at the bus stop by our house. Singing, dancing, and going over our spelling words was part of the start to our day.

Oak Forest Elementary, a small one-story brick school nestled under the tall oak trees on Stanley Road in Nakina, is our fondly remembered school. Since we attended the all-Black elementary school, our books were secondhand and that meant that the books had been used by a white school in the county before they came to us. Old Dock, the white school in Nakina, had used them for two years, and we had to write our names on the third line provided. We took the books home and covered them with grocery bags for protection. Folding the edges and cutting out the back portions to securely tuck properly held your cover in place. We had secondhand materials, and we still came out winners in spite of . . .

Our lineup of teachers left an indelible imprint on us. We remember them, and the hometown from which they came, as if it were yesterday.

- **Grade 1** Mrs. Eula Spaulding Whiteville, NC
- **Grade 2** Mrs. Callie Alston Sedalia, NC
- **Grade 3** Mrs. Carrie Smith Hallsboro, NC
- **Grade 4** Mrs. Mazzie Stanley Nakina, NC
- **Grade 5** Mrs. Mazzie Stanley Nakina, NC
- **Grade 6** Mrs. Mattie Powell Whiteville, NC
- **Grade 7** Mr. Leroy Lawrence Whiteville, NC
- **Grade 8** Mr. Franklin Boone Hallsboro, NC

While our parents gave us the basics and the foundation to build character and become the giving, loving, caring contributors that we have become, our teachers, along with our principal, Mr. Donnie Graham, cultivated principles in us to become a positive, integral part of the world.

So, what are some of the life lessons that we were taught by our parents, our Sunday School teachers, and our elementary school teachers? Here's a list from my perspective:

1. *No matter what, always do your best*
2. *Believe in yourself*
3. *A winner never quits, and a quitter never wins*
4. *Make the most of the 3 R's—reading, (w)riting, (a)rithmetic*
5. *Practice memorization using Bible verses and the Pledge of Allegiance*
6. *Respect yourself and others*
7. *Establish good study habits*
8. *Practice good manners like saying yes ma'am or yes sir, thank you, and please*
9. *Speak with confidence and conviction*
10. *Be assertive versus aggressive to achieve your goals*
11. *Master the English language*

12. *Start each day with a daily devotion*

13. *Dream because the sky's the limit*

One of the things that I have never understood is how it would help in life to learn to diagram a sentence. I know that speaking and writing your thoughts clearly are important, but putting conjunctions, prepositions, adjectives, and adverbs on little lines never did seem helpful to me. Then there were those complex and compound sentences! Did anyone ever use sentence diagramming in the "real world" or corporate America? I'll bet I can guess your answer. An emphatic NO!

At any rate, good or bad, useful or maybe not, we are eternally appreciative of the immeasurable lessons we learned from our beloved elementary teachers. Their imprints will forever be etched into our being. Hats off to our phenomenal teachers and our principal. You loved us unconditionally, as if we were your own kids. Our school was home away from home. Thank God for making us a part of the marvelous orbit!

Now, on to high school—1965.

CHAPTER 5

Nakina High School

A winner never quits, and a quitter never wins.
– Vince Lombardi

The year 1965, the month of August specifically, is forever and always etched into my memory. Why? It was the school year that was optional. We could attend the all-Black high school in Tabor City, a small eastern North Carolina town 20 miles away, or we could elect to go to the school closest to our home—Nakina High School, which had an all-white enrollment.

My sister, Clara, who is two years older than I am, and I chose to integrate the Columbus County school system. Apprehension, anxiety, fear, uneasiness, and trepidation all began to creep in. Our mom, Clara, and I went to the school weeks prior to the start date to meet the principal and teachers and to get our bus assignment.

The first day of school arrived. This is where the rubber meets the road. Our white neighbors, Libby Ward, Clara's age, and her sister, Judy, my age, greeted us with wide smiles and huge hugs as we boarded bus #153. Clara and I took the seat just behind Libby and Judy, glancing around the bus to see reactions of the others. The ride was extremely quiet. But when the bus rolled up to the school and we unloaded, integration truly began.

There were ugly words immediately. "Hello, niggers" and "you monkeys" were some of the words we heard. And "Why are you here?"

I was always one to speak my mind and say exactly what I was thinking at that age, with no filters, and let the chips fall where they may. So, with a group of students now forming around us, I responded, "Obviously you don't know, but this is the year that it is optional for us to make a change. We have the option to travel miles to an all-Black school, or we can choose to attend the school closest to where we live. My sister and I chose to come here because it is closest to where we live."

When someone said that they did not want us at their school, I was quick to respond that we really didn't want to be there as much as they didn't want us there but that they were going to have to deal with it. Tension mounted, the crowd grew, and two teachers, Mr. Boyd and Mrs. Biddix, stood next to Clara and me. What a day . . .

That was just the beginning. After a few days, the name calling slowly came to a halt. However, the stares and snickering continued. Clara and I decided to ignore those acts as much as possible and see how long we could endure. Teachers constantly checked with us to see how we were coping with this overwhelming situation. Our neighbors, Libby and Judy, escorted us or met with us between classes to see how things were going.

The ride home each afternoon was quiet. One young man would sit next to us and eventually sat on the same seat with Clara. They discussed everything from homework assignments to the real issue at hand, our thoughts on integration.

Our mom and our younger brothers anxiously awaited our daily return. We were eager to discuss every encounter of the day. Sometimes Libby and Judy would come over to our house after we got home.

As the weeks passed, things began to get a little better. Mom kept a close check with the principal and our teachers. After settling down and getting accustomed to this new environment, Clara and I decided that we were going to concentrate on our studies and shut out all of the other foolishness. We made straight A's and proved to everyone that skin color had absolutely nothing to do with our intelligence. Clara never missed a day in school. She had perfect attendance from grade 1 through grade 12. However, with asthma, I missed days periodically. When I had an asthma attack, my brother Roy Latson would get a pot of water and put it on top of the wood-fired heater until it produced steam. This would help me breathe more easily. There were no humidifiers back then. Latson was my "angel" during those asthma attacks.

Respect is earned. As months passed, our responses in class coupled with our test results showed teachers and classmates that we learned quickly, we were pretty smart, and we could readily grasp and comprehend lessons just as easily as anyone else, if not more easily.

The following school year was quite different as more Blacks were in attendance. Tension was not nearly as great. Once the white students came to the realization that we were there to stay, Blacks and whites began mingling and communicating. Thank God for dedicated and welcoming teachers. Not all of them were, but the good ones far outweighed the "not so good" ones.

Some interesting things happened in my third year of high school when my brother, Ervin, two years my junior, came to Nakina. One teacher actually grouped all of the Black students in one class. And to make matters worse, the students were further subdivided, categorized by "aptitude." Psychologically, this played with their minds and made them think and feel "less than."

This class was without an actual classroom teacher. These students were never given an assignment, a test, or homework. At the end of the school year, they were all given a "C" for the year.

There were more unbelievable stories during this four-year period. Despite a lack of recognition for talented basketball players—scholarship offers were withheld, for example—to misleading guidance counseling, our people succeeded in spite of it all. We stumbled upon some priceless resources that were instrumental in catapulting us to unexpected landings, and we learned from other sources about applying for full academic scholarships and various financial resources to secure funding for further education.

In 1969, when grade averages were shared for my grade, my cousin had a 93 GPA, a white classmate had a 95, and I had a 97. The principal had a "called meeting" with the three of us along with our parents. He informed us that because the averages were so close, with only a 2-point spread between each of us, he and the teachers decided that I would not be named valedictorian nor would a salutatorian be named, but the three of us would march with honors.

My mom, along with several other parents (Black and white), took the issue to the superintendent, and he said it was totally up to the principal to make the call. My cousin went on to pursue a nursing career, our classmate who would have been salutatorian became a teacher, and I became a television executive.

A hard knock, but these incidents certainly enabled a person to understand and appreciate the fact that no one can prevent you from achieving your potential. With persistence, tenacity, and hard work, and, of course, the undergirding of God's guidance, we can reach for the stars.

CHAPTER 6

College Days

All of our dreams come true,
if we have the courage to pursue them.
– Walt Disney

College days were totally different from anything that I had previously encountered. You were just a number. My first semester at North Carolina Central University (NCCU) was exciting and at the same time somewhat of a blur. Living in a dormitory with hundreds of young women, some friendly and some as cold as ice, communal bathrooms, and three roommates was all foreign territory to me.

Most of the professors were cordial, however, some were stoic with a chip on their shoulder as if they didn't want to be there. One professor introduced herself by saying, "Don't expect any grade higher than a "C" in this class. The author gets an "A" for writing the book. I get a "B" for teaching the class. And you will receive a "C" or below." What an introduction. And she frequently had migraine headaches, which made her extremely irritable and a force to be reckoned with.

During my first semester, my mom suffered a massive

stroke. At this time there were no home health care services in our county. My brothers called and asked if I would be willing to come home and care for Mom. Of course, my answer was yes.

God's grace and mercy, coupled with help from my younger brothers, Ervin and Jerome, and the women in our Nakina community—Aunt Mary, Aunt Dessie, cousins Rhodia, Maggie, Versie, and Alberta, and our Supply cousins, in particular, Mom's first cousin Dorothy—were all angels.

The incidents of this year were nothing shy of miraculous. Mom's recovery was amazing. We were all, especially her doctors, in awe of her daily progress. This ten-month time period taught me many life lessons. At the ripe age of 18, I was nursing my mom back to health, chauffeuring her to therapy and doctor's appointments, cooking, paying bills, and all that encompassed taking care of the household. I would not trade that experience for anything, and you definitely can't put a price tag on love and care. Mom would often say to me, "Because you sacrificed your schooling to take care of me, you will never have to want for anything." She was correct. I have lived a great life with a wonderful career and family, never yearning for anything I did not have.

In September 1970, I returned to NCCU as an advanced freshman. I was in the work-study program, and one of my responsibilities was being a receptionist at the Annie Day Shephard dormitory where I was a resident. While I was working one day, three gentlemen entered through the glass double doors. The most handsome of the three was immaculately dressed and had beautiful hazel eyes. As he tells it, he told his two friends that he was going to talk to the first beautiful young Black lady he saw. Well, the first one he saw was my roommate, China Toodle, who was six foot two. When China stood to get a notepad, he looked back at his friends and said, "She is too tall for me. One of you can talk with her, and I will go a little farther."

When he saw me, he told them, "She's the one." He strode over and introduced himself as Lee Booker, asked my name and classification, and immediately wanted to know what I would be doing after I got off work. I told him that my shift ended at three o'clock and that I had to go across campus to "drop and add" a class. He said that since I was an advanced freshman and he was a big-time senior, he'd be more than happy to accompany me to the gym to take care of my drop and add. I told him he was being quite assertive, and he quickly responded that he was just trying to help!

He waited until I got off work. As we strolled to the gym, he kept telling me that he loved my deep dimples. I was thinking to myself, "*Dude, you are too much!*" We dated for the next three and a half years. As it turned out, from that day to now, we have been the best of friends.

This period of my life was exhausting, but it definitely helped in shaping the person I have become. I had to work exceptionally hard, carrying 18-24 hours per semester, studying every free moment in order to graduate on time with my class in 1973. One of the most rewarding experiences from this time was developing friendships that have lasted from 1969 to the present. I can't begin to list the full spectrum of "life lessons" I garnered during my college years, but here are some of them:

1. *Put your trust in the Lord as it says in Psalm 18:8*

2. *Don't wear your feelings on your sleeve*

3. *Treat others the way you'd like to be treated*

4. *Study*

5. *Keep your nose clean*

6. *Mind your own business*

7. *Don't share your personal issues unless you want to see them published in media*

8. *Pray for those disrespectful to you without reason and be kind to them*

9. *Be cautious with whom you associate—association brings assimilation*

10. *Take time to breathe and to smile—smiling takes fewer muscles than frowning*

I am sure, very sure, that God divinely orchestrates our lives. I met Lee on that beautiful fall day, and he became my best friend, my traveling partner, my confidant, my prayer warrior, and eventually my life partner and husband—oh how blessed am I?

I graduated from NCCU in May 1973 with a Bachelor of Arts in English and a minor in Education.

Climbing the Ladder

CHAPTER 7

Recipe for Success

Success is not measured by your accomplishments, but by the accomplishments you help others to achieve.
– Orison Swett Marden

If I were to address a high school class of 50 students on Career Day at nine a.m., a college class of 100 students at a Motivational Task Force Day at noon, and a room of 50 account executives at a local television station at three p.m. and ask them each to write a paragraph on what the word success means to them, I would receive 200 unique definitions because success means something different to each individual. No matter how you define success and no matter in what stage of life you find yourself, I have laid out my 11 ingredients that I believe will help to ensure your success. I am certain that there are motivational speakers, life-coaches, and mentors who have different ingredients, but these have worked for me:

1. The first and most important ingredient is **GOD**. You must keep God center and first. Any decision that I have to make, no

matter how big or small, I consult with God. Every morning before I get out of bed, I thank God for keeping me through the night and allowing me to see a new day with new mercy, grace, and favor. I also read my Bible, say my prayers, and ask God to divinely orchestrate my day.

In all your ways acknowledge him,
and he will make straight your paths.
Proverbs 3:6

No one can serve two masters;
for a slave will either hate the one and love the other, or be devoted to the one and despise the other.
Matthew 6:24

But strive first for the kingdom of God and his righteousness, and all these things will be given to you as well.
Matthew 6:33

I have discovered in my 69 years of life that it is imperative we keep God center and first if we want to attain success.

I believe this and say it often. God is the reason that I am who I am and where I am. When I think back over my life, God has been divinely orchestrating my steps. From being born to parents who believed in and trusted God as the source and supplier of their needs to attending an all–Black elementary school to integrating the public school system in Columbus County, North Carolina, to attending a historically Black university, all I can say is "but God."

I see God's handiwork in meeting my husband, getting married, giving birth and raising two beautiful, gifted, and God-fearing daughters, and now being richly blessed to have five extraordinary, loving, exceptional grandchildren. When I think of God's goodness and all that He has done, is currently doing, and most importantly, what He is about to do in the lives of His people, my heart leaps with joy.

2. **High Self-Esteem** is important. Jerry Lewis in "*The Nutty Professor*" said, "You'd better learn to like yourself because you are going to be spending a lot of time with you." A beautiful thing about self-esteem is that it grows by feeding upon itself. The better we feel about ourselves, the more likely we are going to get along with others. Without exception, the real winner and highly motivated achiever has accepted his/her own uniqueness, feels comfortable with his/her image, and is willing that others know and accept them just as they are. You must think positively about "you."

This is so true. If you don't believe in yourself, then who will? This is why it is so important to do affirmations often. When you wake up, look in the mirror and say something positive—"I am alive with a reasonable portion of health, activities of my limbs, sight, and today is going to be an awesome day."

Get up, dress up, and show up and always display an "attitude of gratitude." Wear a smile in spite of the negativity that may be going on around you. Smiling is contagious. Feeling great about yourself can completely change the atmosphere of a room.

3. **Vision** is the art of seeing things that are invisible—the ability to think about or plan the future with imagination or wisdom. Other words are imagination, creativity, creative power of seeing, field of vision, and perspective. No doubt you can think of visionaries you know. I often think how our parents, our siblings, our church families, our national leaders (there is so much to be said about President Obama, our first African American president), and our local business owners are visionaries. Jim Goodmon, the president and CEO of Capitol Broadcasting until recently when he turned the helm over to his son, Jimmy Goodmon, is a perfect example of a visionary.

   Speaking of visionaries and Capitol Broadcasting (the company I retired from), there is a quite amazing story of vision related to WRAL-TV. This is the story according to WRAL history.

> In 1939, A.J. Fletcher, founder of Capitol Broadcasting, and his son, Fred, saw a television demonstration at the World's Fair in New York City. Both were fascinated by the flickering pictures on the small oval screen, but TV at the time was still very much a novelty. Fast forward to the early 1950s and post-war America. Sales of TV sets were beginning to boom, and A.J. Fletcher was determined not to miss out on the potential of the exciting new medium. On October 17, 1953, Capitol Broadcasting Company formally applied for a license to operate a television station in Raleigh, North Carolina. With that, the battle for Channel 5 began.
>
> Two companies wanted Channel 5. One was Capitol Broadcasting and the second was the much larger Durham Life Insurance Company, owner and operator of WPTF-AM, the dominant radio station in the region. Since two applicants wanted the same channel, a competitive hearing was scheduled to determine which company was better suited to hold the license. The

proceedings began in Washington, DC, in April 1954 and went on for nine long months. Capitol Broadcasting Company was the decided underdog, but they won the battle with A.J. Fletcher's vision, and the rest is history. (https://history.capitolbroadcasting.com/divisions/wral-tv/)

4. **Technology and innovation** are important ingredients for success. You must stay abreast of changes in this ever-changing global society. If not, you are "left behind." I was proud to be a part of Capitol Broadcasting as the national award-winning company that brought the first VHF television station to Raleigh, North Carolina.

5. You must have a **plan of action**. No matter what stage you are in life, you have to "plan your work, and work your plan." The origins of this saying are unknown, but it has certainly been used by many. People as different as Vince Lombardi and Margaret Thatcher were both known to say this.

   Planning is actually a type of goal setting. There are three kinds of goals: goals based on time, goals based on focus, and goals based on a topic. Time goals are the ones we refer to as short-term or long-term goals to accomplish something. Focus goals remind us of big audacious goals and drive the majority of our decisions. Topic-based goals can be personal, professional, career, or financial. It is imperative that you establish long-term as well as short-term goals.

Check periodically to see where you are in terms of achieving those goals. Habakkuk 2:2 says to "Write the vision, make it plain." What are things that you can do to change your course, or revise your plan of action to help you get where you'd like to be? Keep in mind, you are in charge of "you." It does help to document your plan, your thoughts. Even in retirement, I continue to set goals for myself. Tenacity is a huge factor in staying focused and on track.

Time, focus, and topic goals are not mutually exclusive. We can have short-term financial goals, long-term career goals, and personal focus goals. At Capitol Broadcasting, we had our teams establish SMART plans to achieve goals. This acronym means:

- **S–Specific:** What goals you're trying to accomplish? Be specific.
- **M–Measurable:** How can you measure your success?
- **A–Actionable:** What are the actionable steps needed to achieve the goal?
- **R–Responsible:** Who are the people who must support this goal (work, friends, family)?
- **T–Time-bound:** When do you want to

achieve the goal?

As the saying goes, if you don't know where you are going in life, any road will take you there. If you don't clearly know where you want to go, how will you know when you get there? Planning is the roadmap that guides you to your destination. Motivation is the fuel that gets you there. SMART goals help you with a plan that will lead to desired accomplishments.

6. Be a **life-long learner**. This is what our parents always taught my siblings and me. Once you learn something—get it into your brain (your human computer)—then no one can take that knowledge from you. Learn "by any means necessary" as Malcolm X would say. Reading, watching television, taking free classes, attending workshops, garnering information from others all work to gain knowledge.

   Assess the information carefully for reliability and accuracy. Build your vocabulary. Knowledge is power. In the NIV Bible, Proverbs 24:5 says: "The wise prevail through great power, and those who have knowledge muster their strength." The same passage in the English Standard Version reads: "A wise man is full of strength, and a man of knowledge enhances his might." Each is a slightly different way for rendering the same lesson. It behooves us to learn, learn, and learn some more. School is never out for the highly motivated achiever.

"Knowledge comes, but wisdom lingers," Alfred Lord Tennyson said. We must learn how to learn, because learning is more vital than ever to those who want to succeed in today's new world with its constant economic, political, social, and—the biggest of all—technological changes. Just think of the advances in technology in your lifetime. In order to be competitive and successful, you have to keep abreast of these monumental changes, leading us back to life lesson four!

7. Learn to accept **responsibility**. There are so many references in the Bible about accepting responsibility. For every action, there is a reaction and, ultimately, a consequence. If you have committed an undesirable act, the sooner you accept responsibility, the better off you are, and in some cases, if not all, the lesser the consequences you will face. There are numerous examples of this happening as we listen to the "ever breaking" news in the White House, our nation, our state, and our families. As writer Susan Taylor says in her book *Lessons on Living*, sometimes "it's a sad state of affairs."

Even in biblical days, there was unrest.

Unrest seems more heightened today because of social media and news being repeated over every outlet. In Luke 16:10, we read: "Whoever is faithful in a very little is faithful also in much; and whoever is dishonest in a very little is dishonest also in much." And Galatians 6:5: "Each of you must take responsibility for doing the creative best you can with your own life." That passage continues with verses 7-9: "Don't be misled: No one makes a fool of God. What a person plants, he will harvest. The person who plants selfishness, ignoring the needs of others and ignoring God will harvest a crop of weeds. All he'll have to show for his life is weeds. But the one who plants in response to God, letting God's spirit do the growth work for him, will harvest a crop of real life—eternal life."

8. Make a **good appearance**. Your appearance speaks volumes about you. Whether you are interviewing with a locally owned and operated business or a Fortune 500 corporation, your first impression is a lasting impression. You have 60 seconds to make your first impression and to be sized up completely. Therefore, present your very best "you." Both your preparation as well as your presentation must be impeccable. Looking the person in the eye, not fidgeting, and staying calm and focused are key.

9. **Family** is foundational. Whenever I am talking to students or to adults in a corporate setting, I stress the importance of family. They are your true support system. And no matter how successful you become, don't ever forget where you have come from. A strong family is unbeatable. Most of us would not be where we are today without our family. The sacrifices, and most importantly, the prayers of our parents and grandparents were all integral and major contributors to our success.

10. **Believe in yourself.** There may be days when you get up in the morning and things aren't the way you had hoped they would be. That's when you have to tell yourself that things will get better. There are times when people disappoint you and let you down, but those are the times when you must remind yourself to trust your own judgments and opinions and keep your life focused on believing in yourself and all that you are capable of doing.

    There will be challenges to face and changes to make in your life, and it is up to you to accept them. Constantly keep yourself headed in the right direction for you. It may not be easy at times, but in those times of struggle, you will find a stronger sense of who you are. When the days come that are filled with frustration and unexpected responsibilities, remember to believe in yourself and all you want your life to be, because the challenges and changes will only help you to find the goals that you know are meant to come true for you.

11. **Attitude** makes the difference. I spoke about attitude and choice in chapter two. The longer I live, the more I realize the impact of attitude on life. Attitude, to me, is more important than facts. It is more important than the past, than education, than money, than circumstances, than failures, than successes, than what other people think or say or do. It is more important than appearance, gifted ability, or learned skill. It will make or break a company, a church, a home, a person.

    The remarkable thing is that we have a choice every day regarding the attitude we will embrace for that day. We cannot change our past. We cannot change the fact that people will act in a certain way. We cannot change the inevitable. The only thing that we can do is play on the one string that we have and this string is attitude. I am convinced that my life is ten percent what happens to me and ninety percent how I react to it. And so, I believe, it is with you.

We are in charge of our attitudes.
– Charles Swindoll

CHAPTER 8

Thirty Years in Television

Great companies are built by wise planning. They grow strong through common sense, and they profit wonderfully by keeping abreast of the facts . . .
– Proverbs 24:3 - 5

In April of 2020, all of the news coverage around the world and here in the US was, yes, the *coronavirus pandemic, COVID-19.* The number of cases, hospitalizations, and deaths were alarming, and medical experts predicted more to come. And that came to pass.

Ironically, at that time in our weekly noon Bible Study, we were focused on The Book of Revelation (last book of the Bible). The Book of Revelation sums up the whole of God's dealings with man and with the devil. In this book, the Holy Spirit gave its author, John, the sweeping purpose of God from beginning to end—to completely and eternally redeem man whom the devil had stolen from God, and through His son Jesus Christ, to restore man to everything God created him for, and for the earth to be all God created it to be. God, man, and earth would all be ONE again, this time forever.

Prophetically, so many things are revealed in this last book, which also coincidentally addresses events that are currently happening.

As the coronavirus raged, we found ourselves in a leadership vacuum. According to a quote from an article in *The Atlantic* on April 10, 2020, President Donald Trump spoke in the Rose Garden on March 13, 2020 and said, "I don't take responsibility at all" in regard to the spread of COVID-19. Those words might end up as the epitaph of his presidency, the single sentence that sums it all. Trump fancied himself as the "war-time president."

David Frum, staff writer, shared the following in an article in *The Atlantic* on April 7, 2020. The title of the article is "Americans Are Paying the Price for Trump's Failures."

- By the end of March, the coronavirus had killed more Americans than the 911 attacks.

- By the first weekend in April, the virus had killed more Americans than any single battle of the Civil War.

- By Easter, it may have killed more Americans than were killed in the Korean War.

- On present trajectory, it will have killed, by late April, more Americans than the Vietnam War.

The United States is on track to suffer more sickness, dying, and more economic harm from this virus than any other comparably developed country. This pandemic is a monster that is affecting all of us in one way or another.

One of my nephews sent a text to me on April 7, 2020, which read:

In three short months, just like God did with the plagues of Egypt, He has taken away everything we worship. God said, "You want to worship athletes, I will shut down the stadiums. You want to worship musicians, I will shut down the Civic Centers. You want to worship actors, I will shut down theaters. You want to worship money, I will shut down the economy . . . . You don't want to go to church and worship Me, I will make it so that you can't go to church.

2 Chronicles 7:14 says: "If my people who are called by My name will humble themselves and pray and seek My face and turn from their wicked ways, then I will hear from heaven and will forgive their sins and will heal their land."

Indeed, we need to take this time of isolation from the distractions of the world and have a personal revival where we focus on the ONLY thing in the world that really matters, our Lord and Savior Jesus Christ! Continue to bless God and be a blessing to others.

So how does all of this connect? In a time of great worldwide distress, our media keeps us updated and connected. The world is so interconnected today that we are called upon more than ever to see the big picture—to think globally and see the consequences of action or inaction. I am proud to have been part of the television industry for thirty years that has helped connect the world. I also am a firm believer that everything that happens is divinely orchestrated. Let's start at the beginning and connect the dots of my career path in the television industry.

Assistant Copywriter

In September of 1980, I applied for a position as an Assistant Copywriter with the Production Department, Capitol Broadcasting Company, Raleigh, North Carolina - WRAL-TV and was hired right away. I was the mother of two little ones at the time. As production writers in Creative Services, our responsibility was to produce public service announcements (PSAs), commercials promoting the station, and commercials for mostly local clients.

Sales Assistant

After six months in that position, I accepted a new job as a sales assistant. Once there, I listened and learned everything I possibly could. Working with sales people, clients, and the sales management team was a whole new world for me. There were so many unique personalities and attitudes. My responsibility was to assist the sales team each time they got a new sales order in house.

I began by diligently digging in and learning pertinent terminology. I learned about terms like DMA (Designated Marketing Area), Rating and Share, HUTS/PUTS (Homes Using Television/Persons Using TV) Reach, and Frequency Demographics Dayparts. It was a whole new language in my new world!

In addition to all of the paperwork, a colleague and I would periodically deal with clients regarding make-goods. Make-goods were done when the station, for one reason or another, missed the originally assigned program or when there was an under delivery of promised ratings/shares. A perfect example of this was when 9/11 occurred. So much of our programming was preempted because of this tragedy, through no fault of the station. Stations chose not to air certain commercials during this crisis out of decency and respect for lives lost.

I'm a quick study, and I very much enjoyed my work in this role. Many clients also clearly enjoyed working with me. They often told me that I was so easy going, always explicit in my explanations, fast and efficient with paperwork, and great with everything I did. Management often echoed those sentiments, and soon management suggested that I should consider becoming a sales account executive.

Account Executive

After hearing these positive comments on a regular basis, I decided to go for it, never having sold anything EVER! I drafted a memorandum to the management team listing ten reasons I could be, and should be, their next account executive. They created a "trainee" position, hired me, and the rest is "her-story."

Sales is one position where compensation is commensurate with your efforts. If you work hard, you make a significant salary.

There were other rewarding parts of the job too. One of the most rewarding parts of my job as an account executive was to sell a schedule/promotion and to make sure it ran smoothly. The next step was to get all of the in-house responsibilities accomplished. This meant working with Creative Services through the production of the commercial, ensuring that the commercials were properly scheduled, and fulfilling the most critical step—assuring the commercials aired completely. This was all trickier than one might imagine, but I thoroughly enjoyed working with my clients and my colleagues to make all this happen.

During the process and each cycle of TV commercials, it was crucial to always follow up with clients to discuss the impact that their schedule was having on their foot traffic and business. My clients were pleased with their investments and the payoff and thrilled with the results of successful schedules aired on WRAL. They frequently sent letters to station management praising my professionalism. Clients not only told my bosses how much they enjoyed working with me, they shared details of our successful partnership with other potential prospects. Success, as they say, breeds success.

Helping clients use the most effective sight, sound, motion, and emotion medium, and in my view, the best TV station, to increase foot traffic and ultimately boost sales for their business was gratifying. When my clients experienced the positive flow in traffic and reached projected revenue goals that, in turn, yielded longer commitments from them.

I learned generating new business as well as maintaining existing client relationships, coupled with hard work, persistence, tenacity, and drive made for great salesmanship. I was named "Salesperson of the Month" numerous times and Salesperson of the Year four times during my career at WRAL-TV. My name is still on display on plaques at the station.

Senior Account Executive

In 1993, I was promoted to Senior Account Executive. Each time, I took on a new regional account, I gained more and more regional and national sales experience. While I loved my new position, working in corporate America was not always a bed of roses, a walk in the park, or smooth sailing. There were several occasions where I almost lost my cool. No matter what, all Account Executives (AEs) are expected to maintain composure at all costs. I added to my life lessons during this time.

While I was fortunate to work with many exceptional people in my career with CBC, as with any company, there was the occasional bump with a boss. An example of this was when management decided to step on toes or override the sale of one of their AEs for another client or for their own benefit. I did not experience this often, but it did happen more than one time. Sparks can fly in situations like this as you can imagine!

My boss added a competitor's commercial right in the middle of a "special program" that was sponsored by one of my major clients. This was done at the very last minute, without my knowledge or my permission. You can imagine how that conversation went with my manager before I alerted my client. I made it crystal clear that whether my client, who was understandably furious, paid for the special or not, I expected to be compensated for the entire contract total.

And the "dirty tricks" weren't limited to those kinds of tactics. The same colleague had a repertoire of mean "jokes" and belittling remarks that were frequently deployed, mostly on female staffers. One habit was to immediately page a person if there was no answer when she called an extension. Never mind that we all spent a lot of time on the phone with clients! Unfortunately (maybe for both of us), I was one of the all too frequent recipients of this "sense of humor"—if you could call it humor.

I requested vacation days in 1990 to hear Nelson Mandela speak in Atlanta shortly after he was freed from prison after 27 years. I wanted to take my two young daughters, and my brother Ervin, who lives in Atlanta, was going to join us. I requested two days off just a few days prior to my trip. I felt these were extenuating circumstances.

When I made my request, this colleague wanted to know where I was going "last minute." I explained it was personal. I took off Friday and Monday. She persisted in asking, and ultimately discovered that I was going to Atlanta for the Mandela gathering.

Upon my return on Tuesday morning, I heard a page

"Winnie Booker, please call 8791." I did not respond. A few minutes later, I and everyone heard "Evelyn Mandela, please call 8791." I was livid. I immediately got up from my desk, walked swiftly down the hall to her office, and closed the door. I pulled the guest chair as close to her chair as I could get, and my exact words were, "As long as you are white and I am Black, don't you ever, ever refer to me as anyone other than Evelyn Booker. Is that clear?"

My boss was startled, sat back in her chair, turned beet-red and said, "I am so sorry. I was only teasing you to let you know that I found out why you made a last-minute vacation request. I apologize and I promise you, it will never, ever happen again." Staff said that they had never seen me so angry. To cool off, I drove from our Western Boulevard office to our corporate office on Hillsborough Street to speak to our HR Director.

There are so, so many other instances of this employee's racist and sometimes malicious "teasing" that only she found amusing. Here's another example. On the morning of my 40th birthday, there were signs on all the windows at work that read "Lordy, Lordy, EBO is 40." EBO is my computer name, and it always stuck. The sales staff had planned a fun party with gag gifts, real gifts, cards, and refreshments. The card from this colleague was the menu from the Golden Agers' luncheon, an event that Capitol Broadcasting held annually to recognize seniors in our community. Fresh cantaloupe, watermelon, and honeydew were items on the menu. She circled watermelon and wrote, "You know how you and your people like watermelon." I made a copy and took it over to HR for both our permanent files. This made me even more determined to "win in spite of . . . "

Was this 30-year journey an easy one? ABSOLUTELY NOT. But my determination knows no bounds!

One morning as I was leaving a meeting, the Creative Services department was in the sales conference room to critique their most recent commercials produced for the month. I was asked by the department head if I could join them as they watched. We were to reserve comments until the entire reel was over.

As people began giving their comments, both positive and negative, the department head asked for my feedback. I asked if Blacks buy cars, eat food, wear clothes, or make doctor's visits. Everyone looked at me in amazement. I proceeded to tell them that there were no Blacks in any of the commercials.

The response was to the effect of "Wow, we had not thought of that!" Then I was asked if I knew of any Blacks who would be interested in doing commercials. Of course I did, and so the process began and moved forward. Blacks were included in that "pool of talent."

LSM to GSM

Several years later, and much to our surprise, Capitol Broadcasting Company (WRAL's parent company) entered into a local marketing agreement with Channel 50, originally owned by Tar Heel Broadcasting and known as WACN and decided to build a new television station in Raleigh. When I learned that a totally different team, separate from WRAL-TV's sales team, would be selling the station, I decided to apply for the new Local Sales Manager (LSM) position. With some coaching from a colleague and a couple of the WRAL team members, I put together a presentation detailing my experience, my name in the industry, and the reasons why I was the best candidate for LSM, bar none, to lead the sales team. I always seek God's divine guidance when making a decision, big or small, and considering this move was no exception. I was hired for the position.

On September 7, 1995, the station signed on as WRAZ. When I learned that the station was seeking a General Sales Manager (GSM), I jumped at the opportunity. I felt that my years of experience in sales and with the company would certainly make me a prime candidate for the GSM position. I was promoted, and we began breaking records.

Motivating a team of awesome gifts, talents, and personalities is no small feat. Drive varies. It comes from within, sometimes maybe with heredity, and sometimes is acquired. What is the common thread that keeps a team all headed in the right direction?

As we've all heard many times, there is no "I" in the word team, therefore a real team is a group of like-minded individuals working together for the same goal. The key ingredient to getting and keeping your group motivated is simple, though granted not always easy. Positive attitude + enthusiasm = success. When you give positive feedback and constantly display an "attitude of gratitude" for efforts made, hard work is inevitable.

As I often say, success breeds success. Successful people motivate and encourage success in each other. While I always enjoyed working with my team, motivating and encouraging them, one of the most grueling responsibilities as a manager was doing bi-annual and annual employee reviews, a 16-page report ordeal.

Reviews made for an interesting exchange between our employees and their managers. Employees were given the opportunity to do a "self-review," in essence "grading themselves" in the same categories as we graded them. The seven behaviors upon which they were graded were interpersonal communication, attitude toward company and work, resourcefulness, job competence, initiative, dependability, and judgment. We had goal setting—divisional goals, departmental goals, and key responsibilities—specific to each individual's goals. The fact that employees and managers compared and discussed all categories made for a solid, sound, respectful relationship.

I also traveled often in my job. We had offices throughout the US and periodically visiting those offices with our GM and National Sales Manager was taxing but extremely exciting as well as gratifying. TeleRep was our rep firm, and they played a huge role in our national revenue, while our Local Sales Manager along with the team of Account Executives managed our local client base.

On one of my first trips to New York, I had to address our team. I talked to them about six ways to stay motivated, the importance of keeping themselves in great shape mentally, physically, and emotionally, and what we could do as a team not only to make budget but to exceed budget.

One of the representatives raised his hand and said that he wanted to thank me. He said this was the first time that a GSM had talked to them about their personal well-being. Usually everything was about budgets. There was a loud round of applause.

And did they perform? Yes, indeed.

Another exciting moment during my career was being elected to the FOX50 Network's Sales Advisory Committee. Capitol afforded me the opportunity to attend the committee's annual meeting in New Orleans, where two others and I were formally appointed to a two-year term. I was in charge of the "Atlanta Two" region that included ten stations in the southeast. The SAC committee conferenced once a month, sharing sales ideas and other network related business issues. This post offered two benefits: the election was a benefit to me for industry exposure and networking, and it was a huge benefit for FOX50 because of the many unique and non-traditional ideas that were shared for developing new business. It was a pleasure and an honor to serve on this committee.

An exceptional period on this 30-year journey was when our General Manager had to take a 10-month medical leave. The CEO of Capitol Broadcasting, Jim Goodmon, asked if I would act as interim GM. I thought about it, prayed, and accepted the challenge. It was a fascinating experience, a time of exponential growth, and an eye-opening glimpse into another sphere of management, responsibilities, and accountabilities. I was so fortunate to receive extraordinary support and endorsement from the community, advertising arena, our clients, and the staff, who were especially remarkable in stepping up to help.

So how do you move a team from "good" to "great" to "phenomenal"? You must have a plan of action, vision, expectations, and ultimately, a means to an end. You must make sure that your entire team has buy-in, is a part of, and shares the vision/goals.

Each year we had a sales planning session, and everyone on the team contributed. I planned the agenda (with input from team members) and selected an off-site venue. All participants had ample time to prepare for the role they would play on stage and, most importantly, the contributions each would make in achieving or exceeding expectations for the coming year.

One year our theme was *We Will Play to Win*. We set SMART goals, reviewed the local and national budgets by month, looked at projected revenue sales, and laid out a strategy for the upcoming year with everyone playing a part.

In my experience, I have found the following to be very effective for building a successful team:

- Involve your team in the entire planning process
- Hold every player accountable
- Compliment jobs well done
- Encourage on-going training
- Hold weekly sales meetings
- Share both successes and issues encountered from previous week
- Invite motivational or inspirational speakers
- Build in monetary incentives
- Hold dinners and give gifts for making budgets
- Show sincere appreciation

In 1998, WRAZ's main offices and master control relocated to the Diamond View office building in downtown Durham next door to the Durham Bulls Athletic Park and the American Tobacco complex. In 2000, Capitol Broadcasting bought WRAZ outright. In most markets, such a duopoly would not have been allowed under Federal Communications Commission (FCC) rules, which forbid one company from owning two of the four largest stations in a single market.

When we first signed on as FOX50, some of our WRAL-TV's sales team teased us, calling us "Just 1's" FOX, meaning that we were generating low ratings of "1." Did that change quickly? I kept a diary of my years in television, and we made history *having our first million dollar month in September 1998.* We had more million dollar months thereafter.

What a team we had in place! One of the most rewarding and enjoyable parts of my job was hiring brilliant, hard-working, grateful employees. That makes the difference. That *is* the difference. We broke all kinds of records not only for making but for exceeding sales budget goals. This enabled us to take our clients on yearly incentive trips to places like Casa De Campo, Las Vegas, and Dominican Republic.

Another phenomenal experience during my tenure at Capitol Broadcasting was being selected to go to Detroit, Michigan, and spend a week with the authors of the Crucial Conversations course. Crucial Conversations is such a powerful class and experience. It teaches us to be able to speak to anyone, at any time, regarding any subject without feeling there would be repercussions.

When I returned from Detroit, I was thrilled to be among a select few to teach the 16-hour course to all employees of the company. So many employees had been intimidated by or afraid to talk with management. After participating in Crucial Conversations, this problem was alleviated in our organization. I also went to Wilmington, North Carolina, to teach the two-day class to the eight radio stations owned by Capitol.

The letters of thanks that followed this program were incredible. Several employees said that the course improved their personal life as much as their professional life. Completing the Crucial Conversations class is a significant achievement to add to any portfolio. Thanks go to Capitol Broadcasting for making this course available to all employees and ensuring a more cordial work environment for everyone.

Lessons garnered in Crucial Conversations are lessons and skillsets for life. Three things stood out in particular to me:

- When dealing with people, take all of the emotion out of the situation and just deal with facts. It's hard to argue against facts.

- Everything starts with *you.*

- You can control the direction that any conversation takes.

I encourage you to take the Crucial Conversations course if given the opportunity. It changes lives.

While it was an honor to have been chosen to teach this course to the employees of Capitol Broadcasting (approximately 520 at that time), all of my usual responsibilities were still there. Managing and motivating the sales team, attending "Motivational Task Force" days at the area colleges and universities, being involved in the community, and most importantly, making budget were all in a day's work.

CHAPTER 9

CRACKING THE GLASS CEILING

Victory is not the absence of problems.
It is the presence of God's power!
– Greg Boyd, The Gospel Coalition

I don't typically get nervous about many things, but when Sabrina Jones, a staff writer with the *New & Observer*, called and said she'd like to interview me, all kinds of nervous energies crept in.

I must admit I had never been interviewed for a newspaper article, even though there was an article written about my sister Clara and me when we integrated the Columbus County school system in 1965. This would be different. Ms. Jones said it would be very casual, and her staff photographer, Jim Bounds, would be with her to take a few photos in my daily work environment.

And so it happened on a cold winter morning in January 2000. One of the questions Ms. Jones asked me was what was taught to me as a youngster from my parents that still has meaning today. My answer was they instilled in all their children that we would have to work twice as hard for half the recognition and that whatever we did, always give it 100 percent of our efforts.

Were they correct? You'd better believe it!

I also shared with Ms. Jones that after six months of employment with WRAL-TV and learning as much as I could, I sent a letter to management listing ten reasons I could and should be an account executive on their sales team. In 2000, there were not many African Americans in the television industry. I distinctly remember the interview with the station manager. After a series of exchanges, he asked me if I felt being African American and female would negatively impact my performance on the team. I responded that I considered both to be assets, positives, and that WRAL clients were interested in one color—green—and how WRAL's reach could bring them more customers. I told him that the client's bottom line was what kind of return they could expect from their investment.

Then I asked him (at the suggestion of my brothers Archie and Ervin, who were sales executives/managers with IBM) how I stacked up relative to the other applicants, and if he had to make a decision today, why or why not, would I be his top candidate. That question took him by surprise (as my brothers said it would). After all, *he* was interviewing *me*. The ultimate decision was that I was their top candidate, and I was hired for the position.

In the article written in 2000, Ms. Jones wrote that by 2006, women would make up 47 percent of the nation's workforce, and she predicted that by 2050, minorities would make up nearly half of the nation's population. She also quoted Karen Jayson, a North Carolina employment security research analyst, who felt that as the labor market tightened, women and minorities would move into higher positions.

Now take a look at the statistics two decades later, from 2000 to 2020. In an article published July 1, 2020, a *USA Today* analysis reports that

> . . . while corporations and board rooms have added African Americans over the decades, the executive suite has not—even at companies that have diverse boards. Nearly all—48 of the 50 largest companies—issued statements in support of the Black community following George Floyd's death on May 25, 2020, in an unprecedented outpouring after decades of corporate silence on anti-Black racism and police killings in the United States. Companies across the country have been speaking out against racism, but fewer than 2 percent of the 279 top executives at those 50 largest companies are Black. Of those 279 top executives listed in the proxy statements (regulatory filings to help stockholders make informed decisions at stockholder meetings), only five, or 1.8 percent, were Black, including two who recently retired.
>
> Many of the mega-companies are still led solely by white executives in the top five slots listed on proxy statements: the CEO, the chief financial officer, and three other top-paid executives. Business and diversity scholars say the executive suite is still one of America's most exclusive and impenetrable clubs, with the corporate hierarchy most closely resembling a plantation: heavily white at the top and Blacks struggling to move up.
>
> ***— USA Today, August 20, 2020,***
> ***Jessica Guynn and Brent Schrotenboer,***
> ***Why are there still so few Black Executives in America***

In "They Spoke Up about Racial Injustice, Now What . . ." in *USA Today*, August 2020, Jessica Guynn and Brent Schrotenboer wrote:

> For decades, corporate America has failed to hire, promote, and fairly pay Black men and women, stalling many from rising above middle management according to Smith. This stark racial divide has a cascading effect, stagnating income levels and helping worsen the race, class, and wealth gap that is yawning even wider during this COVID-19 pandemic. It also puts corporations at a disadvantage. As the nation gets less white and more diverse, corporate America will need to adapt to better serve that changing market. A 2018 Boston Consulting study suggests that greater diversity on leadership teams improves financial performance and innovation. Even small changes to senior teams can generate gains, the study found.
>
> Ella L. J. Bell Smith is the co-author of *Our Separate Ways*, which examines the career trajectories of Black and white female managers. Smith's message to corporate America in 2020 is "move beyond the hashtag activism. The reality is that we have to get past talking." She continues, "How many times do you have to hear how women of color, men of color, are being ostracized in your company? How many stories from Black folks do you need?" Some companies spoke up about racial injustice. Now what?
>
> On May 30, Netflix's corporate Twitter account tweeted: "To be silent is to be complicit. Black lives matter, we have a platform, and we have a duty to our Black members, employees, creators, and talent to speak up." Co-CEO Reed Hastings and his wife, Patty

> Quillin, also announced they were donating $120 million to historically Black colleges and universities to reverse generations of inequity in our country. Numerous stories came from Netflix, Nike, Apple, Providence Equity, Time Warner, Verizon, Amazon, Microsoft. JP Morgan Walmart, Bank of America, Cisco, Oracle . . . and the list goes on.

I encourage you to read the stories in *The Road Ahead* by Bill Gates and read articles by Lonnae O'Neal, senior writer at TheUndefeated.com.

Being a woman in corporate America comes with its fair share of challenges. Often women face gender discrimination and bias in the workplace. But if you're a Black woman or woman of color, these gender-based challenges are often compounded by obstacles of racism, making it even harder to navigate your way to the top. According to the National Partnership for Women and Families, "Even among Harvard MBAs – few Black women ever reach America's top rungs."

In her July 1, 2020, article on CNBC.com titled "How corporate America's diversity initiatives continue to fail Black women," Courtney Connley wrote, "Currently there are 37 women leading Fortune 500 firms, a new record and an increase from last year's record high of 33. Of these women, just 3 are women of color and none are Black or Latina. When looking at the total workforce in the US, Black women account for 7% of the population but make up 12% of the minimum wage earners. We all must lean in on this to correct the situation."

The question I pose is what can we do to change this narrative?

CHAPTER 10

Induction into the YWCA Academy of Women

Whether you think that you can, or whether you think you can't, you are right.
– Henry Ford

One of the most exciting, memorable moments of my career was to be nominated by our General Manager, and ultimately to be chosen, for induction into the YWCA's Academy of Women, class of 2006.

Among other goals, the YMCA empowers women and works to eliminate racism. The YWCA of the Greater Triangle has supported close to 1,800 members and volunteers and provides services for nearly 15,000 women and their families across the Triangle.

In 1983, the annual Academy of Women awards event was created by the YWCA of the Greater Triangle to recognize the achievements of outstanding local women. Inductees have demonstrated a commitment to the YWCA's mission to empower women and eliminate racism. My induction was such an exciting and exhilarating evening.

Capitol Broadcasting had 3 tables of employees and many of my family and church family also attended. Being able to talk with the other inductees in our Class and learn about them as individuals and their respective roles in the community gave each of us a totally different perspective regarding the roles women play in our varied industries. Despite differences, we are interwoven by our similarities.

The YWCA Academy of Women

is an honorary society formed in 1985 under the auspices of the YWCA. It is comprised of women who have been formally inducted into membership through their singular achievements in a specific discipline. The 2006 inductees are:

Eleanor Jordan
Arts & Entertainment

Evelyn Smith Booker
Business

Barbara B. Volk
Community Service

Gladys Fowler Graves
Education

Beverly Murray
Entrepreneur

Polly H. Leousis
Exercise & Sports Fitness

Linda Coleman
Government

Lou Mitchell
Health & Human Services

Joanne Kurtzberg
Professions

Enriqueta Bond
Science & Technology

Kelly Collins
Teen Woman

CHAPTER 11

Passing the Torch

The river is within us, the sea is all about us.
– T. S. Eliot

Tenacity, drive, persistence, and hard work certainly ring true in the typical day and week of a general sales manager (GSM). My days always began in full speed ahead mode. After devotion and quiet time prior to the commute, I would prepare myself mentally for the day. Getting into the office well in advance of my team afforded me the opportunity to prepare for the day.

Once my team began to arrive, it was "Katie bar the door" or better "Evelyn bar the door." That's what made the job of GSM so incredibly awesome. From dealing with a team of varied personalities to clients from all walks of life to working with other divisions within our company to community involvement to representing Capitol at various colleges and universities in the area during Motivational Task Day or Week, it was all amazing. I found it quite refreshing to talk with young, brilliant minds as they were nearing college graduation, polishing their resumes, and interviewing to land their first job in the real world or in corporate America.

I regularly prepared various sales performance reports to share with management regarding what our local, regional, and national teams had pending and our projected finish. I met with local account executives if our LSM was out of the office and met weekly with all our managers and the promotional manager for routine business and to address any issues or challenges from the past week or upcoming week as well as to determine topics to discuss at the next sales meeting. There always was something interesting going on!

Political seasons were challenging, yet interesting months. Pricing the station, accommodating candidates on both sides, dealing with preemptions, and keeping the political file open and accessible to the public during work hours while abiding by all the local, state, and national political guidelines made us all scratch our heads and breathe an enormous sigh of relief to see each November 2nd at noon come around.

Department head meetings plus meetings with creative, sales, traffic, promotion, inventory, and TeleRep (our national rep firm) were all weekly occurrences. I had a bell that we rang when there was a big sale, new business, an increase in a business order, a switch/pitch (a sale in which we garnered dollars from the competition), or an annual order. All were reasons to celebrate. The bell was loud enough that all departments would come over to sales to hear the success story. The responsible party, the one who made the sale, took center stage to share the details.

The quarterly market audit gave a snapshot of our revenue. Revenue from local, regional, national, and political (during political seasons) markets were reflected in the data. The markets covered included Atlanta, Charlotte, Nashville,

Florida, and Richmond, Virginia, for local and national covered New York, Dallas, Chicago, Philadelphia, Boston, and selected accounts in Atlanta and Los Angeles.

My responsibilities also included those bi-annual and annual reviews that I previously mentioned for our sales assistants, local, regional, national and traffic managers.

My days were full for thirty years. Then it was time for me to pass the torch, so I began my succession plan. I prepared a detailed daily, weekly, monthly, quarterly, annual accountabilities report for our General Manager and corporate to guide my successor.

On March 11, 2011, I retired from Capitol Broadcasting. It was a bitter-sweet moment! The celebration that FOX50 gave for me was "off the charts." Over 300 people attended. It was an exciting event, full of recalling memories of the past thirty years and creating warm goodbye memories. My family, my church family, TeleRep managers from all over the country, former managers, friends from college, and former employees were there to celebrate with me. What a night! Words are inadequate to express my sincere gratitude for the efforts of the staff of Fox50 in planning and orchestrating such a special evening. Life is good, and hard work pays *huge dividends*. Our WB/FOX50 team rocked!

I owe a huge debt of gratitude to many people at Capitol Broadcasting who were instrumental in my growth and success. As John Donne wrote in his devotions in 1624, "No man is an island." I am so appreciative for my collective community, God first and then my parents, family, and my corporate family. I thank each of you because I could not have done it without you.

Here are a few of my memorable accomplishments at Capitol Broadcasting:

- 1980 September. . . . .Began my career at Capitol Broadcasting
- 1981 March . . . . .Sales Assistant, WRAL-TV
- 1981 September. . . . .Account Executive Trainee
- 1982 April . . . . .Account Executive
- 1993 September. . . . .Promoted to Sr. Account Executive
- 1996 October. . . . . . .Promoted to Local Sales Manager - Warner Brothers
- 1997 May. . . . . .5 Star Award - Employee of the Year
- 1997 July 27. . . . . . . .Volunteer Excellence Award
- 1997 September. . . . .General Sales manager - Warner Brothers
- 1998 September 22 . .1st Million $ Month
- 2004 July 21. . . . . . . .Completion of Crucial Conversations Mastery
- 2004 July 23. . . . . . . .Crucial Conversations Certified Trainer
- 2005 June 17 . . . . . . .Supervisor Training (EAP in Supervision)
- 2005 September 25 . .Leadership Coaching Trainer
- 2005 October 21 . . . .Capitol Broadcasting Managing for Performance Leadership Edge
- 2006 April . . . . .Manchester's Who's Who Executives and Professionals
- 2007 May. . . . . .Cambridge's Who's Who Executives and Professionals
- 2008 October 15 . . . .Vitalsmarts - Influencer Trainer
- 2010 March 4 . . . . . .National Association of Professional Women
- 2011 March 11 . . . . .Retirement

CHAPTER 12

Paying It Forward

Live your life in such a way that you'll be remembered for your kindness, compassion, fairness, character, benevolence, and a force for good who had much respect for life, in general.

– Germany Kent

When your character is built on a spiritual and moral foundation, your contagious way of life will influence millions.

– Martin Luther King, Jr.

Here's a question to ponder. What impact have you had on people with whom you have come in contact? Was the impact positive? For me, an important part of my life's work has been to try to mentor and help others. This was part of the life lessons my parents instilled in my siblings and me. I was humbled by the comments penned by my first hires at Capitol Broadcasting Company when they shared the impact that I had on them and their careers. They were a joy to work with, and I am so proud of them. They each moved on to larger markets, garnering greater experience, and, I'm happy to report, also substantial incomes. Here are five letters I received with permission granted to include them in this book. I include them not only because their words warm my heart but also, and primarily, because the power of mentoring is so clear and they are paying it forward!

> *There are times in one's life when they are at a loss for words; this would be one of those times for me. Not because I have little to say, but because there are not enough words to explain the profound influence of Evelyn Booker. To me she will always be EBO, my mentor, my friend, and the person that inspired me to carve out my unique path to success. When you step back and evaluate her gifts, you will see intelligence, poise, professionalism, and an unshakable determination to bring value to every task and every person she encounters. She has persevered through times when the advertising and broadcast industries were dominated by white men who begrudgingly "let" women into client facing roles, but were still resistant to "allow" black women into leadership roles. Evelyn is a refined force of nature. She did not need anyone to "allow" her the opportunity; she earned it.*
>
> *I came from a blue collar, low-income family. I wanted more for my life. I was driven to prove everyone wrong and overcome any impediment to my success. When I saw an obstacle, I wanted to clear it and then kick it down in the process. It took me many years to master the greatest lesson she ever taught me. She encouraged me to always stay in the fight but be strategic about the weapons I used. Instead of focusing on tearing down the obstacle, she inspired me to simply reach back over the wall and help someone else clear it. Eventually there would be enough of "us" on the inside to shift the balance of power, so the next*

generation of women (of every color or economic status) would not have to constantly prove that we deserved a seat at the table. Evelyn Booker is not a person that is afraid of confrontation; she is brave beyond measure. Her strength lies in her ability to outthink the opposition.

In doing so, she wins over the majority and becomes a power too big to resist. Anyone who has ever worked for her knows they are a better person and professional because of her guidance. She is a role model in every sense of the word, but when I think of EBO, I think greatness. Not just her greatness, but the greatness she inspires in everyone she meets. I was a diamond in the rough. Evelyn Booker told me I could shine, and I believed her. I owe much of my corporate success to this amazing woman. Way before the country had Michelle Obama, I had Evelyn Booker, as did so many of her direct reports after me. We are a family of connected strangers, all privileged to have worked for and learned from the wisdom of a first-class lady.

Heather Colley
Higher Education Marketing Technology
Atlanta, GA

~

What Evelyn Booker Means to Me:

My name is Leon Duncan and I am Senior Vice President of Hospitality and Entertainment with the Washington Redskins [Note: currently known as the Washington Football Team].

The day I went to work for Evelyn Booker marks one of, if not the most, pivotal moments in my life.

She was so much more than a boss to me. She was my mentor, my relationship counselor, my spiritual advisor and my moral compass.

In order for one to be great, there has to be a certain level of self-belief. Once I moved on from broadcast sales into working in professional sports with the Washington Redskins, I found myself working for an organization comprised of some of the most talented and goal-oriented individuals I had ever seen. Of course, I was a bit intimidated at first—but it didn't take much time for me to settle in and thrive.

Evelyn Booker had instilled the confidence that I needed to do great things. "If you think you can or if you think you can't—you're right!" Evelyn would always use that line whenever a member of her team seemed to be facing what was perceived to be an insurmountable challenge. I took that with me and even to this day I share it with my kids whenever they allow some of life's challenges to get them down.

After 5 years with the Redskins, I went on to become a Brand Director at Under Armour which was one of the fastest growing companies in the country at the time. UA bolstered a roster of some of the most talented athletes in the world including Michael Phelps, Tom Brady, Steph Curry, Bryce Harper, Jordan Spieth, Ryan Zimmerman, and Cam Newton to name a few. Whenever the opportunity presented itself, I would ask an athlete to sign an autograph for my son which always included the message "If you think you can…"

Every night when I used to tuck my son into bed, I would put my hand on his chest and say it. His response was always the same "Royce Frasier Duncan can do anything!"

Leon Duncan
SVP Hospitality & Entertainment
Washington Redskins
(now the Washington Football Team)
Washington, DC

~

Meeting Evelyn Booker was an important part of my journey in this life. She not only mentored me in the business world but also in my personal life. Her nurturing spirit guided me, and she was like my second mom. She would call me her "cream baby," which confirmed that our relationship was deeper than employer/ employee. Evelyn's influence in my life has had a profound impact on who I am today.

We met when she interviewed me for a sales position at a new TV station in Raleigh, North Carolina, WRAZ TV. I was a spunky single mom who needed some guidance, and I was seven hours away from my parents. For my chaotic existence, her peaceful presence was a welcome and much needed addition to my day-to-day life. She shared the mantras, "If you think you can or if you think you can't, you're right" and "You win some, you lose some, and some get rained out." Those statements have guided me in so many situations throughout my life.

Evelyn is a God-fearing woman, and I loved the training and advice that she would give me regularly, because I knew that someone bigger was guiding her. She taught me all the basics of relationship building, sales, communication, parenting, and life.

We always had fun until she hired a bunch of boys,

who I'm sure have messages in this book as well. I'm just kidding, Kevin, Leon and Cameron! She had a knack for hiring incredible talent because we all went on to do great things! I believe that it was that nurturing nature that made her one of the best mentors and managers I've ever had, and I'm so proud that she considers me one of her own! Love you, EBO!!!

Kendall Hartel
Broker, EXP Realty
Raleigh, NC

~

I am honored to have the opportunity to express gratitude and to be able to tell anyone who will listen how important Evelyn Booker is to the universe.

My name is Cameron and I am a successful sales executive in New York City for a large media company. How I got to where I am now is directly linked to where I started, which was my first sales job in Raleigh, NC, with Evelyn. The start she gave me, and what I learned from her was pivotal. I didn't know it then, but it would serve as the footing for the professional I am today.

I was a typical 22 year old, I suppose, who thought they knew everything. I relied on charm more than substance and hard work. Evelyn took me on as a project because she saw something in me. She coached, inspired, and motivated. She gave me the foundational tools to develop a skill set that stands the test of time. She had the unique ability to tie humanity to the profession, so despite your desire to be great in a competitive environment, you were principled, which means you'd do it "the right way." We could use more of that today. Evelyn was tough and she held me accountable. I believe that, as much as anything, was the biggest building block for me.

I learned the meaning of hard work. I didn't know how to apply it then, but because I had Evelyn as my mentor, I could hear her as my career advanced. She's been hugely impactful on my life in so many ways, and I'm thankful I was fortunate enough to train under her.

I think it's worth noting, particularly in this moment, Evelyn's story in her own career is incredibly relevant. Her story is arguably more significant now, and I reference it often now that I'm in a position to hire, mentor, and promote. Her legacy is creating a new crop of black leaders, and I hope she's proud of that.

Cameron Poston, Sr.
Director of Sales
NBC Regional Sports Network, NBC
New York

~

If you are a college basketball fan over the age of 40, you likely know the name Dean Smith who coached Michael Jordan and many other Hall of Fame players at the University of North Carolina. Coach Smith was not only a coach during their time in college but became a life-long mentor to his players. Michael Jordan and others rarely made an important life decision without consulting Coach Smith. Evelyn Booker is my Coach Smith.

Evelyn was the one who hired me out of college and thus was my first professional boss. Her impact on my career is immense, and I could not have had a better teacher. Evelyn taught the importance of "the little things." While most know to do the key tasks expected, but to distinguish yourself, you also need to focus on the small details. Overall, Evelyn believed in outworking the competition. No matter what a competitor's approach, Evelyn would go beyond it every time.

When you combine Evelyn's humble spirit, her genuine care about a client's needs, and her unmatched work ethic, the result was a person who was the absolute best at what she did. This was my mentor. This is the person who taught me everything she knew—holding nothing back. It is undeniable that the root of my success is Evelyn Booker.

As a person, we've often described Evelyn as an angel on Earth. She is the most caring and supportive person I've met and has an uncanny "direct dial" to God as everything she prays for seems to come to fruition. She's also someone who integrated her high school and has overcome countless stereotypes as an African-American woman in the South. It's difficult to overstate the impressiveness of Evelyn Booker.

Since working for Evelyn, I've remained in ad sales working in Washington, DC, Philadelphia, and New York. I've managed a team of 30+, I've worked in local and global sales, I've managed hundreds of millions of dollars in ad revenue, and with every job, in every city, with every step along my career path, I've relied on the teachings and foundation given to me by Evelyn Booker. She taught me about life, about sales, about humble competition, and instilled in me a spirit of service and gratitude.

Because of Evelyn, I approach each day with the confidence of knowing I learned from the best. Whether

I'm talking to the CMO of a Fortune 500 company or an intern in my office, I know if I hold true to the teachings of Evelyn Booker, the result will be positive and fruitful, leaving an impression that they've encountered someone different from the rest. That's the lasting imprint of Evelyn Booker and why I'll forever be grateful for her presence in my life.

Kevin Hungate
Vice President, NBC News Ad Sales
NBC Universal

~

I hired Aolani Donegan as a sales assistant after she was highly recommended by one of our managers. Aolani was an exceptional and exemplary employee and an incredible writer. While employed, she did further studies to earn her undergraduate degree from East Carolina University. She got married, had two sons, and is now pursuing a Master's degree at UNC-Chapel Hill while working a full-time job. With her permission, I'm sharing what she wrote for my retirement celebration:

March 24, 2011

Even though Jackie Robinson may have smashed cultural barriers to play for the Brooklyn Dodgers . . . he had nothing on you.

Evelyn, just like Jackie's sacrifices paved the way for young baseball players, you have opened doors and supported so many of us in this room.

Arthur Ashe, even with all his Grand Slam titles—his single wins at Wimbleton, the US and Australian Opens still . . . has nothing on you. You are the best at what you do and you won't quit until you know how to find that report or drop a photo into something you are working on. To be successful in sales you have said it requires tact and skill, much like tennis and golf.

EBO—you have given us all the tools to be able to hit "ACES" when the ball is in our court. We promise not to forget all the lessons and I promise to hem my pants moving forward! =) You make time for everyone—even if you are in the middle of quarterly reports, you say "Come in—give me a minute." It means a lot to know when you turn to face us, we have all your attention and you genuinely care about the outcome.

I am grateful that I got to come to WRAZ from 99.9 FM and "getting to" work for you has been one of the best things in my adult life. I will miss the smell of Lee's homemade sweet Honey BBQ sauce before share builders on a Tuesday. Thank you for always offering me a hush puppy. We've been lucky to have your time for all these years—now it's your time . . .

In Hawai'ian, we say ALOHA 'OE. It means farewell . . .

But the cool thing about Hawai'ian is that ALOHA means hello and goodbye. But most of all it expresses LOVE.

So FOX50 family, please raise your glass to EBO . . . ALOHA!!!

Aolani Donegan

Things Need to Change

CHAPTER 13

A Sad State of Affairs

Whenever you do a thing,
act like the whole world is watching.
– *Thomas Jefferson*

Though COVID-19 is raging in the world as I write this book, this is not our only concern. In the US, we have been fighting systemic racism for hundreds of years. Many have lost their lives. Black men are particularly vulnerable. In 2020, thousands of people took to the streets protesting individual Black deaths. While the events included in this chapter are by no means inclusive, events, legislation, and actions presented are representative. *US News/The Guardian* published an extensive list of well over 100 of these violent acts. The initial article titled "Young Black Men Killed by US Police" was published December 15, 2016 and then it was updated July 22, 2020. The writers are Jon Swaine, Oliver Laughland, Jamiles Lartey, and Ciara McCarthy. Below I have summarized a few of the alarming, widely and well documented laws and violent events affecting Black people.

Statutes between 1864 and 1957

Between 1864 and 1957 statutes were enacted that impacted many lives.

- Three Jim Crow laws passed between 1864 and 1908, all concerning miscegenation.
- In 1908, Oklahoma passed a miscegenation law that banned marriage between those of African descent with those of non-African descent.
- In 1876, there were statues barring school segregation.
- That was followed by ending segregation of public facilities in 1885.
- Four laws protecting Civil Liberties were passed between 1930 and 1957. Miscegenation was repealed.

Tulsa Race Massacre

On May 31 and June 1, 1921, Black residents, their homes, and businesses were targeted in the Tulsa Race Riot. This was also referred to as the Greenwood Massacre and the Black Wall Street Massacre of 1921. For two days white mobs attacked Black residents and businesses of the Greenwood District in Tulsa, Oklahoma. An entire neighborhood of affluent people of color was totally destroyed.

Tuskegee Airmen

Tuskegee Airmen were the first African American soldiers to successfully complete their training and enter the Army Air Corp (Army Air Forces). In 1948, almost 1,000 aviators were produced as America's first African American military pilots. There were 66 Tuskegee-trained aviators killed in action during WWII and another 32 became POWs after being shot down. Instead of being greeted with a hero's welcome at their eventual return home, the Tuskegee Airmen were segregated as soon as they disembarked the ships that brought them home. German prisoners of war were treated better than Black Americans. In 1948, President Harry Truman signed Executive Order 9981 that imposed equality of treatment and opportunity in all US Armed Forces.

Emmett Till

Emmett Till, a 14-year-old African American from Chicago, was brutally murdered in Money, Mississippi, for allegedly flirting with a white woman. The woman's husband and her brother made Emmett carry a 75-pound cotton gin fan to the bank of the Tallahatchie River. They ordered him to take off his clothes, then the two men then beat him nearly to death, gouged out his eye, shot him in the head, and threw his body, tied to the cotton gin fan with barbed wire, into the river.

The Civil Rights Act

The Civil Rights Act of 1964 was a landmark Civil Rights and Labor Law in the US that outlawed discrimination based on race, color, religion, sex, or national origin. This Act prohibits unequal application of voter registration requirements and racial segregation in schools, employment, and public accommodations.

The Voting Rights Act of 1965

The Voting Rights Act of 1965 was signed into law by President Lyndon B. Johnson with the aim to overcome legal barriers at the state and local levels that prevented African Americans from exercising their right to vote under the 15th Amendment to the United States Constitution.

Trayvon Martin

On February 26, 2012, a 17-year-old African American high school student named Trayvon Martin was fatally shot in Sanford, Florida, by George Zimmerman, a Neighborhood Watch captain. Martin was walking in his own neighborhood. He was wearing a hoodie. He'd been to the 7/11 store and had purchased Twizzlers and a bottle of tea. Zimmerman was acquitted in July 2013.

Eric Harris

April 2, 2015, Robert Bates, a 74-year-old volunteer sheriff's deputy, claimed he confused his 38-caliber handgun for a stun gun and accidentally shot Eric Harris after Harris fled a sting involving a gun sale. Harris was unarmed. In video footage, a single shot is heard and a voice saying, "I'm sorry, I shot him." Harris says he cannot breathe, and a voice responds, "(Expletive) your breath." Bates received a four-year sentence in 2016, but he was released in October 2017.

Walter Scott

On April 4, 2015, police officer Michael Slager shot Walter Scott in the back five times as Scott fled. Scott was unarmed. A broken tail light initiated the encounter. Slager placed a taser next to Scott's body and later claimed Scott had tried to taser him. A federal judge sentenced Slager to 20 years in prison.

Emanuel African Methodist Church Slayings

Dylann Roof shot to death nine African Americans during a Bible Study at the Emanuel African Methodist Church in Charleston, South Carolina, on June 17, 2015. The next morning Roof was arrested in Shelby, North Carolina. He targeted members of this church because of its history and stature. In December 2016, he was convicted of 33 federal hate crimes and murder charges. Though he was sentenced to death for these crimes on January 10, 2017, he pleaded guilty to all nine state charges in order to avoid a death sentence. He received a life imprisonment for each charge. Roof published a website manifesto before the shooting and wrote a journal from jail afterward. On January 4, 2017, Roof wrote that he "would like to make it crystal clear, I do not regret what I did."

Alton Sterling

Three-hundred-pound Alton Sterling was selling CDs outside a convenience store in Baton Rouge, Louisiana, on July 5, 2016. Officers Howie Lake and Blane Salamoni approached him following a report of a man with a gun. Sterling was wrestled to the ground because the officers said he refused an order. Salamoni initially shot Sterling three times, claiming Sterling reached for a gun in his pocket. When Sterling tried to sit up, Salamoni fired three more shots into his back. Sterling, a convicted felon, was illegally carrying a gun. In March of 2018, a state attorney general announced no charges would be filed against either officer.

Philandro Castile

Philando Castile was killed in Falcon Heights, Minnesota, on July 6, 2016 by officer Jeronimo Yanez, who claimed he pulled Castile for a broken tail light. Later it was determined through radio calls that Yanez thought Castile resembled a robbery suspect. Shortly after Castile informed Yanez he had a gun in the car (for which Castile had a permit), Yanez shot Castile twice in the heart. Castile's girlfriend live-streamed the killing's aftermath on Facebook. Other bullets fired narrowly missed her. Yanez was found not guilty of manslaughter in 2017.

Terence Crutcher

Betty Shelby, a white Tulsa police officer, fatally shot Terrence Crutcher on September 16, 2016. She called the unarmed Crutcher a "bad dude." His hands were up as he stood near his vehicle in the street at the time of the shooting.

Ahmaud Arbery

Ahmaud Arbery was a 25-year-old Black man out jogging in Brunswick, Georgia, on February 23, 2020. He was fatally shot by a white father-son duo.

Breonna Taylor

Breonna Taylor, a 26-year-old emergency medical technician, was at home asleep on March 13, 2020, in Louisville, Kentucky. Police entered the apartment where she was sleeping by using a battering ram on the entry door. She was fatally shot by Louisville police who were at the wrong apartment in a search for two men allegedly dealing drugs.

The Amy Cooper Incident

Amy Cooper, a white woman, was walking her dog unleashed in an area called the Ramble in Central Park in NYC on May 25, 2020, when she encountered Christian Cooper, a Black birdwatcher. Cooper asked her to leash her dog as is required in that area. She said, "I am taking a picture and calling the cops." After a brief confrontation, Amy Cooper called 911 and said that a Black man was harassing her.

George Floyd

George Floyd, a 46-year-old Black man, was killed in Minneapolis, Minnesota, on May 25, 2020, during an arrest for allegedly using a counterfeit $20 bill. Derek Chauvin, a white police officer, knelt on Floyd's neck for almost 9 minutes, while Floyd was handcuffed, face down. Floyd repeatedly said, "I can't breathe." Officers J. Alexander Kueng and Thomas Lane further restrained Floyd, while officer Tou Thao prevented bystanders from intervening. Chauvin did not remove his knee until medics instructed him to do so.

Rayshard Brooks

Rayshard Brooks, a 27-year-old Black man, was shot and killed by Atlanta police on June 12, 2020. Atlanta Mayor Keisha Bottoms called this an unjustified use of deadly force. Brooks had fallen asleep in his vehicle and was blocking the drive-through of a Wendy's. A scuffle with police officers ensued and Brooks grabbed the officer's taser. He was shot twice in the back as he was running away.

~

From routine daily events like going to the doctor, sending our babies off to school, going for a walk or jog, driving a car, or going shopping, there is a major difference in how Blacks are greeted and treated. When we look at these United States of America, all one can say is this is a sad state of affairs.

During Dr. Martin Luther King, Jr.'s "I Have a Dream" speech, on August 28, 1963, during the March on Washington for Jobs and Freedom, one of his many profound statements was "*I have a dream that my four children will one day live in a nation where they will not be judged by the color of their skin, but by the content of their character.*" If we could put this into practice, we would not be dealing with the extreme issues confronting us daily.

If I were to address all of the recent incidents, it would

consume my entire book. These few that I have mentioned touch us all, whether as a parent, sibling, or just a decent human being.

One of the biggest take-a-ways from the Crucial Conversations course I mentioned earlier was, in any given situation, always take the emotion out of the conversation and just deal in facts. So, following are some facts from *The Guardian* in the form of distressing statistics:

- The final total of people killed by US police officers in 2015 shows the rate of death for young black men was five times higher than white men of the same age.

- Young black men were nine times more likely than other Americans to be killed by police officers in 2015, according to the findings of a *Guardian* study that recorded a final tally of 1,134 deaths at the hands of law enforcement officers this year.

- Despite making up only 2% of the total US population, African American males between the ages of 15 and 34 comprised more than 15% of all deaths logged this year by an ongoing investigation into the use of deadly force by police. Their rate of police-involved deaths was five times higher than for white men of the same age.

- Paired with official government mortality data, this new finding indicates that about one in every 65 deaths of a young African American man in the US is a killing by police.

"This epidemic is disproportionately affecting black

> people," said Brittany Packnet, an activist and member of the White House task force on policing. "We are wasting so many promising young lives by continuing to allow this to happen."
>
> In the same week that a police officer in Cleveland, Ohio, was cleared by a grand jury over the fatal shooting of Tamir Rice, a 12-year-old African American boy who was carrying a toy gun, Packnett said that the criminal justice system was presenting "no deterrent" to the excessive use of deadly force by police. "Tamir didn't even live to be 15," she said.

- Overall in 2015, black people were killed at twice the rate of white, Hispanic and native Americans. About 25% of the African Americans killed were unarmed, compared with 17% of white people. This disparity has narrowed since the database was first published . . . , at which point black people killed were found to be twice as likely not to have a weapon.

www.the guardian.com/us-news/2015/dec/31/ the-counted-police-killings-2015-young-black-men

March 31, 2020, an article on NewsOne.com reported that shooting and killing Black males has been happening for centuries in the US. The sad fact is that it is still thriving in 2020 and only seems to be gaining momentum. This should give any American citizen pause as an increasing number of Black people—especially males both young and old—continue to be added to a growing list of victims with what seems like a new shooting every week.

The article shared these two events:

Ariane McCree

Ariane McCree was detained for allegedly shoplifting at a Walmart in South Carolina on November 23, 2019. Police claimed that the 28-year-old man was placed in custody, then fled, and showed officers a gun. McCree's family claims that he was handcuffed, with his hands behind his back, when he was fatally shot. They have filed a wrongful death lawsuit.

Miles Hall

Miles Hall, 23 years old, suffered from mental illness. Hall's family called for help as a precautionary measure because he was running through the neighborhood "behaving erratically." Walnut Creek Police in San Francisco, California, confronted Hall, who was carrying a long pry bar. When the police called to Hall to come to them, he ran toward them and when he was ordered to stop, paused and then changed directions. Hall was fatally shot on June 2, 2019. His family filed a wrongful death lawsuit alleging that his civil rights were violated.

www.newsone.com/playlist/black-men-boys-who-were-killed-by-police, 3/31/2020

Amina Khan, *LA Times* staff writer, wrote:

> One of the most distressing parts of this seemingly non-stop string of police killings of Black people is the fact that more times than not, the officer involved in the shooting can hide behind the claim that they feared for their lives—even if the victim was shot in the back, as has become the case for so many deadly episodes involving law enforcement. In a handful of these cases—such as Antwon Rose, a 13-year-old boy killed in Pittsburgh and Stephon Clark, a 22-year-old killed in Sacramento, both

> of whom were unarmed—the officers either avoided being criminally charged altogether or were acquitted despite damning evidence that the officers' lives were not threatened, and there was no cause for them to resort to lethal force or any violence for that matter.
>
> ***Amina Khan, Staff Writer,* LA Times**
> ***www.latimes.com/science/story/2019-08-15/police-shootings-are-a-leading-cause-of-death-for-black-men, Aug 16, 2019***

The list seems endless, and my heart aches to see all of the senseless deaths in situations that could have been handled differently.

The question of the century is how do we change this narrative?

In 1963, Sam Cooke wrote a song "A Change is Gonna Come." If by chance you have not heard this song, I encourage you to listen to it. It is imperative that our country alters its treatment of our fellow man. It all starts with me, with you, with heart. If we could simply follow the Golden Rule and treat others the way we'd like to be treated, what a wonderful world this would be.

Connections

CHAPTER 13

Treasured Roles

"For I know the plans I have for you", declares the Lord, "plans to prosper you and not to harm you, plans to give you hope and a future."
– Jeremiah 29:11

As I had many roles in my corporate life that I truly valued, I also have been privileged to have many treasured roles in my personal life.

Daughter and Sibling

The Smith household was a busy household. Because I was asthmatic and could not work outside the house, my main responsibilities in the summer included helping with house chores by doing the laundry and hanging clothes on lines outside. There were no clothes dryers. There were three lines for me to hang the clothes on: whites on one line, lights on the second, and darks on the third. When the clothes were dry, it was my job to get them off the lines and do the folding and ironing. My chores also included helping clean and prepare vegetables to be frozen for the winter months and assisting Mom with preparing breakfast, lunch, and dinner.

Summer months for my siblings often meant getting up early. Their jobs included topping and suckering tobacco, looping (threading it on sticks) for curing, removing the sticks from the barn, transporting the tobacco to the pack house, and then preparing to do the process all over again.

Prepping the cured tobacco to be taken to the market was a big ordeal. Did you know tobacco is graded by color before it is ready for the market?

Grade	**Color**
1	*Light brownish, yellow, or brownish lemon*
2	*Light brown*
3	*Brown*
4	*Dark brown*

Each pile was divided into their appropriate grades. One leaf was placed around the top of a half handful of leaves, all neatly stacked, with that folded leaf tucked in half to make a neatly wrapped bow at the top. The four types were placed in a burlap sheet, ready for the market. It was a treat to go with our parents to the market to sell the tobacco and to witness the reward from all of that hard work.

In addition to the tobacco, my sisters and brothers were responsible for gathering corn, feeding the farm animals, harvesting peanuts, and milking the cows. Slaughtering the hogs was a full day's job and a neighborhood extravaganza.

However, when school was in session, homework was the most important task for all of us.

Our parents were extremely proud of us, and they were always complimentary of our efforts. However, reprimands were in the mix when we did something wrong. One of the things that I admired most about our parents was that they showed no preferential treatment. They stressed the importance of respecting each other for our uniqueness and supported our college choices. They taught us about valuing family and, equally importantly, showing unconditional love. They were beyond their years exhibiting wisdom at its finest and sharing their wisdom generously.

Working so closely with Mom since I could not do the outdoor work made for a special bond between us and gave me my very first lesson in managing up and down being in the eighth position on our family team. I am very blessed to have had these lessons early in my life.

The second lesson from Mom was the importance of setting goals. In order to manage expectations, you have to establish what those expectations are. These two lessons will remain with me for life. Now you can see why I reference goal setting so strongly in my Recipe for Success!

Our parents were God-fearing people and taught all of us the importance of living a Christian life, which meant committing our life to Christ. Most churches now have baptism pools, but then the dipping for the ceremony was done at Reeves Ferry in Nakina. The Reeves Ferry location was quite a beautiful location for baptisms.

Wife, Parent, and Grandparent

Lee and I dated for more than three years after we met when I returned to NCCU as an advanced freshman. On September 1, 1973, we were united in holy matrimony and began our own history. From living in a one-bedroom apartment in Vartimann Gardens in Southeast Raleigh to building our home on a one-acre lot given to us by Lee's parents, we've had an incredible journey so far. We celebrated our 47th anniversary on September 1, 2020.

On September 12, 1975 at 12:50 p.m., God blessed us with a gorgeous baby girl we named Millicent Candene. And on June 1, 1979, at 6:55 p.m., an equally beautiful baby girl graced our world. We named her Eulonda Lea. Both our daughters were born on a Friday, and it was pouring rain for each grand entrance.

Giving birth is one of the most fascinating, miraculous experiences of my life. There is no comparison that expresses the emotional ride you encounter during those nine months of pregnancy. When this precious jewel comes through that birth canal, is wiped down and swallowed in a soft blanket, then placed on your chest next to your rapidly beating heart, the feelings are indescribable. It still brings tears to my eyes when I think about those two moments in time.

Our daughters attended their local elementary and high schools, making friends that are still in their circle today. They furthered their education and are productive, contributing citizens. They truly make us proud to be their parents. These two wonderful young ladies are building their stories from their own perspectives. To see them now as wives and mothers working in this ever-changing global society is so delightful. It is the makings of a true legacy.

Being a grandparent is magnificent. My husband and I are in a totally different space physically, mentally, emotionally, financially, and most importantly, spiritually. Through life's experiences, it would be phenomenal if I knew 30 years ago what I know now. Of course, that is not how it works because "life happens" and not according to our schedule or timetable. We are all witnesses to the fact that the best laid (made) plans by mice and men are apt to go astray. However, we still have to "plan our work, and work our plan" both personally and professionally. According to John 9:4: "We must work the works of Him who sent Me while it is day;

night is coming when no one can work." Work your plans in retirement too!

A Servant in Community and Church

It is such a rewarding feeling to know that you were instrumental, in some small way, for shaping the paths of individuals—some young, some older. Having lived in the Fuquay-Varina, North Carolina, area for the past 47 years, I have seen a lot of growth and many changes, mostly positive and some negative. When our daughters were younger, I served on the Fuquay Varina Area Education Foundation. I felt it was imperative for parents to get involved in the school system, to be fully aware of the expectations of administrators, parents, political figures, and students in particular. I still feel that way today about that parental involvement. Your children, the principals, and the teachers need to know that you are there for your children. You are an integral part of the support team.

Teaching Sunday School while our daughters were in elementary and high school afforded me the opportunity to study and learn more about the Bible. In 2 Timothy 2:15 we are told: "Do your best to present yourself to God as one approved by Him, a worker who has no need to be ashamed, rightly explaining the word of truth." Teaching these young minds each Sunday was no small feat for Sunday School teachers. Those lessons have made a tremendous impact on the lives of these treasured individuals. Many, I might add, have gone on to be business owners, managers, doctors, lawyers, teachers, well-rounded, and well-respected human beings. Of course, most of the credit goes to their parents.

I have been privileged to serve in several positions at church. I currently belong to the deaconess ministry, a position because my husband is a deacon. The deaconesses assist the deacons in preparation of communion and accompany them in visiting members of our congregation who are in the hospital, nursing homes, or convalescent homes. Sadly, because of COVID-19, we are not currently able to make those visits.

I also am an active member of the Ladies Aide Ministry. Our goal is to devise means to raise funds for financial assistance for aiding the community in any area needed (as determined by the ministry), including granting scholarships and making contributions to the church. We've purchased hymnals, a piano, commissioned a mural of the baptism of Jesus by John the Baptist, and sponsored youth trips. We also have an ongoing scholarship fund to assist college aspirants in our church.

Currently, I serve on the board of directors for Healing Transitions, a non-profit recovery service. Our mission there is to offer innovative, peer-based, recovery-oriented services to those individuals with alcoholism and other drug addictions, and our vision is to treat addiction as a health issue. We never turn anyone away who is seeking help because recovery can't wait. Our program is specifically designed to rekindle a person's desire and ability to return to a meaningful and productive life.

It is truly a moving experience to attend one of the awards ceremonies and see "participants" earn their "silver chip" and have their friends and family there in attendance. The statistics are impressive for the ones who have completed the program since its inception.

Serving on the Board of Directors for the Cultural Arts Society of Fuquay Varina has been an eye opener. It is a 501-c-(3), established in 2004, governed by a board of 17 directors, who are unpaid volunteers. We are an active member of the Fuquay-Varina Chamber of Commerce, and we have a sixteen-year history of successfully conducting festivals and Martin Luther King, Jr. celebrations.

On April 27, 2019, we held our first international cultural festival, hosting a diverse assortment of live performances, food and drink, and writers and artisans displaying their works. The celebration was packed with talent from across the world representing African American, African, Caucasian, Asian, native American, Russian, Hispanic, East Indian, South American, Scottish, German, and European cultures—Around the World in Fuquay-Varina was a day of excitement and a chance to learn new things about other cultures!

According to Galatians 5:13: "For you were called to freedom, brothers and sisters; only do not use your freedom as an opportunity for self-indulgence, but through love become slaves to one another." There are so many references in the Bible relative to servants/service, so we are expected to serve others, and God will do the rewarding. It is more blessed to give than to receive. And it boomerangs back—tenfold.

Evelyn, Lee,
and daughters
Eulonda and
Millicent

Millicent
and family

Eulonda
and family

The Booker Family

The Smith Siblings

A "compiled" photo of Smith Siblings (left to right):
Front row: Clara Vaun, Esther, Ethel, Evelyn, Jerome.
Second row: Roy Latson, Rufus, Ervin, Thurman, Henry.
(Deceased: Leamon, Novella, and Ruberta)

The Booker Siblings

(Left to right) Front row: Lee, Dorothy, Elijah,
Second row: Evelyn, Brenton, Harold (not shown, Ralph, deceased)

Smith Family Reunion 2014

Honoring Aunt Mary

CHAPTER 14

Family – Love & Loss

Families are a link to the past and a bridge to the future.
– R. W. Hart

Life is short, so live each day as if it were your last, without frenzy, without apathy, without pretense.
– Emperor Marcus Aurelius

Have you ever wondered how some people who have had terrible beginnings or traumatic events during their life beat the odds and achieve success in spite of it? Is there a secret sauce or are there characteristics that make it possible for individuals to make it "in spite of"? All the members of my family have been successful. To what do we attribute our success? The chapter "Recipe for Success" addresses some thoughts on this, but keeping God center and first, coupled with qualities that our parents instilled in us like integrity, tenacity, drive, honesty, and treating others the way you'd like to be treated all come into play.

If you were to research, there are 33 Bible verses about family, which is also one of the seven spokes in Zig Ziglar's Wheel of Life. Psalm 133:1 says: "How good and pleasant it is when kindred live together in unity!" And Colossians 3:20 says: "Children obey your parents in everything, for this is your acceptable duty in the Lord."

Merriam-Webster defines family as "the basic unit in society traditionally comprising two parents rearing their children, or a basic social unit consisting of parents and their children, considered as a group, whether dwelling together or not, or a social unit consisting of one or more adults together with the children for which they care."

That definition leaves out the important ingredients of belonging and love. I recall all of the emotions when Lee and I began our family—joy, love, fear, compassion, relief, and lots of maternal instincts—but mostly, there was a look ahead with great anticipation of all the things that might happen during the lifetime of each of these miraculous beings that God has blessed, anointed, and appointed to be in our lives, our space, our hearts.

You bring this bundle of joy home and reality sets in—all the responsibilities and accountabilities that accompany parenting. There are all kinds of parenting books, but nothing is 100 percent applicable to your situation. So much is truly trial and error. Thank God for common sense, wisdom, and especially the angels that were assigned to me and to you at birth.

When I think of God's grace, mercy, and favor, my heart, soul, and spirit rejoice at His agape love. He divinely orchestrates life, even before we commit our lives to Christ and develop that intimate relationship that He desires with us. To witness that special gift, we only have to watch a child grow from an infant to toddler, enter daycare, preschool, kindergarten, grades 1-12, and on to the next stages of life that might include jobs or further education, possibly marriage, the beginning of adult life and even perhaps starting the next generation.

I think often of my childhood and the values and principles that our parents instilled in us. They will forever be a part of my siblings and me. We are passing those same values and advice on to our children and grandchildren.

People come into your life for a season or a reason, and some for a lifetime. We are a product of our environment, our family, and more. We love our children unconditionally. We try desperately to pass along those values and character traits that make for a good human being. Life happens along the way. That's a book within itself.

The love, sharing, and caring exemplified by close-knit families make it extremely difficult when there is loss, because there is pain, hurt, and sadness.

The older you are, even though it seems impossible, the more devastating the emotions; and the more piercing the emptiness when a loss occurs. The void left will never be filled. Laughs, sound advice, and fellowship are now memories. However, the comfort and peace that we can hold on to from our faith can ease the pain a bit. According to 2 Corinthians 5:8: "Yes, we do have confidence and we would rather be away from the body and at home with the Lord."

While we miss our loved ones terribly in their passing, as believers, we believe we will see them again in our glorified bodies. What a day of rejoicing that will be. And when we all see Jesus, we will sing and shout the victory. Family members who precede us in death leave an everlasting, indelible mark. Their legacies live on. More importantly, they would want us to continue to live life to the fullest. Death is only a part of this cycle of life.

Each loss is unique. If you have lost a dad, mom, sibling, or someone close to you, you can identify with the severe emptiness their passing leaves. My family has experienced many losses of loved ones. I want to share a very special happening in my life that I believe was to prepare me for yet another loss.

In March 2019, about three weeks prior to the death of my brother, Archie, I was awakened about three-thirty in the morning when a well-dressed gentleman wearing a stingy brim hat was standing by my bed. I kept hitting my husband to wake him up because a man was in our room. The man spoke softly and said, "Evelyn, don't you recognize me?" As I looked under his hat, I said, "Daddy, it's you!" He said that he just came to let me know that everything was going to be okay. I swung my legs off the bed and said that I had a lot to tell him. He smiled, turned, and walked away. As he was leaving, I could see he had wings.

I can still see that image so vividly. It was an experience that I will never, ever forget. For some, I know you have to see it to believe it, but I am saying, yes, I definitely believe in angels.

Over the years my family has received many beautiful cards, telegrams, and letters during our losses, but one poem especially touched my heart.

I Felt an Angel

I felt an angel near today, though one I could not see
I felt an angel oh so close, sent to comfort me.
I felt an angel's kiss, soft upon my cheek
And oh, what a single word of caring did it speak.

I felt an angel's loving touch, soft upon my heart
And with that touch, I felt the pain and hurt within depart.
I felt an angel's tepid tears, fall softly next to mine
And knew that as those tears did dry, a new day would be mine.

I felt an angel's silken wings enfold me with pure love
And felt a strength within me grow, a strength sent from above.
I felt an angel oh so close, though one I could not see
I felt an angel near today, sent to comfort me.

Author Unknown

I have shared a bit of my life's journey and successes with you, but in this chapter about love and loss, I want to share two recent family member losses. The pain was greater because the losses were so close together.

The year 2019 was an emotionally challenging year. Our sister, Ruberta, passed on February 16, 2019, 15 days before her 86th birthday. Ruberta graduated valedictorian of her class in 1952 and graduated from Fayetteville State Teacher's College in 1956. She taught elementary school for ten years in Nakina (how incredibly awesome is it to have your sister teach at the school you attended) before moving to Detroit in 1966, where she was an elementary school librarian in the Detroit Public School system. She completed her master's degree in Library Science in 1974.

Lee and I flew to Detroit for Ruberta's Celebration of Life services. There was snow on the ground and forecasts for more snow. I spoke on behalf of the Smith family about her love for family, her dedication and commitment to kids, and the phenomenal care given by her son, Greg, during her last years. This poem expresses my feelings of loss and hope from her passing.

God's Promises

When sorrow comes
God's promises are shining rays of hope
That breaks through cloudy skies
to bring us warmth and help us cope.

He promises to love us
and to hear our every prayer,
To comfort us and guide us
and to always just be there.

He promises to give us strength
to weather any storm,
To be someone we can lean on
who will keep us safe and warm.

God will never leave us alone
when skies are gray,
As long as we believe and trust,
His love will light our way.

Author Unknown

On March 21, 2019, two days prior to Archie's 74th birthday, our brother earned his heavenly wings. Archie accomplished so much during his 73 years. Our dad died in June 1961 when Archie was only 16. After Dad's untimely death, Archie assumed the role of head of household for the younger siblings. Shirley, Archie's wife, said, "Archie had the most loving family, and they all gave him the love and respect that had come with being the patriarch of their family in their earlier years. They called each other frequently and enjoyed family gatherings with the love and zest that most would find enviable."

Archie earned his B.A. degree in Mathematics at the D.C. Teacher College and his MBA at Pace University in New York. He had well over 40 years of leadership experience.

He entered into a partnership to formulate the KAG Corporation, a product distribution and management support for various commodities. His biggest love was that of real estate investment.

Archie was a member of the Connecticut Chapter of the National Guardsmen, and a charter member of Delta Nu Boule. Both organizations consist of highly educated, influential men, many of whom are millionaires. At the service, they were there, dressed in black tuxedos, white shirts, and bow ties. A representative spoke on behalf of the groups in reference to Archie's contributions. Archie was also a member of Alpha Phi Alpha Fraternity, and they did likewise. I spoke on behalf of the family. Here is a poem that sums up Archie's impact.

In Memory of Archie:
A Journey Remembered
April 12, 2019

As some people journey through life,
They leave footprints
wherever they go.
Footprints of kindness and love, courage and compassion,
humor and inspiration,
joy and faith.
Even when they're gone,
we can still look back and clearly see
the trail they left behind—
A trail bright with hope that invites us to follow.

Evelyn Smith Booker

When I think of all of my siblings and the lessons or knowledge they each taught us about life, this wisdom is priceless—a generous and compassionate spirit, far above rubies!

Things come full circle. You raise children, you teach the same lessons you were taught, you educate them, and they start their families, and so the cycle begins all over. Life is like a song. It's up to you and your heart to write the lyrics to it.

A speech that has really resonated with me is Jim Valvano's inspiring words at the ESPYS awards ceremony on March 4, 1993. He said that there were three things we all should do every day:

- Laugh every day.
- Think; spend some time in thought.
- Cry—have your emotions moved to tears, which could be tears of happiness or joy.

Our time is short and time is precious, so we should strive to make it worthwhile. In our journey, we can accomplish much. If we think we can, we can! The night of his speech, he was announcing the Jimmy V Foundation for Cancer Research whose motto is Don't give up, don't ever give up. Regularly think about:

- Where you started
- Where you are now
- Where you are going
- Where you want to be

In his ESPYS speech, Valvano said, "... cancer can take away all my physical abilities. It cannot touch my mind, it cannot touch my heart, and it cannot touch my soul." So carry this with you. Illnesses can take away physical and mental abilities, sometimes quickly, sometimes slowly, but as Coach Valvano reminded us, our soul remains.

SHARING

EPILOGUE

A Beautiful Life

The events I shared in It's a Sad State of Affairs are both sad and terrifying. I know many people live within these circumstances every day. That makes me all the more grateful for my life. I have worked hard, and I know I am blessed. I have to say, all in all, I know I am so fortunate to have a beautiful life.

I've written a little about my own journey, summarized events describing what has happened and continues to happen to Black people in our society here in the US, and shared some recent losses in my family. As I have moved from phase to phase in my life, I have learned lessons, beginning with my parents, siblings, and school teachers and on through my career and life in general. I've tried to absorb the good and not accept the bad, and I have tried to share what I learned as I learned it along the way with others on their own journey.

My faith has been a strong guide all my life. It has helped me to be a better person and create my beautiful life. To close this book, I am sharing a few simple resources with you. This I know: if your physical, mental, emotional, spiritual, and financial areas are all in alignment, you will be "a better you." All that does not come by accident. It comes through purpose and planning your work and working your plan.

The following pages hold a poem, lists, examples, a little advice, and a touch of home-spun humor to help make your life more beautiful. I hope you enjoy and benefit from them!

Scriptures I Love

The Whole Armor of God

11 Put on the whole armor of God, so that you may be
able to stand against the wiles of the devil.
12 For our struggle is not against enemies of blood and
flesh, but against the rulers, against the authorities, against
the cosmic powers of this present darkness, against the spiri-
tual forces of evil in the heavenly places.
13 Therefore take up the whole armor of God, so that
you may be able to withstand on that evil day, and having
done everything, to stand firm.
14 Stand therefore, and fasten the belt of truth around
your waist, and put on the breastplate of righteousness.
15 As shoes for your feet put on whatever will make you
ready to proclaim the gospel of peace.
16 With all of these, take the shield of faith, with which
you will be able to quench all the flaming arrows of the evil
one.
17 Take the helmet of salvation, and the sword of the
Spirit, which is the word of God.
18 Pray in the Spirit at all times in every prayer and
supplication. To that end keep alert and always persevere in
supplication for all the saints.

Ephesians 6:11-18

Assurance of God's Protection

1 You who live in the shelter of the Most High, who abide in the shadow of the Almighty,[a]

2 will say to the Lord, "My refuge and my fortress; my God, in whom I trust."

3 For he will deliver you from the snare of the fowler and from the deadly pestilence;

4 he will cover you with his pinions, and under his wings you will find refuge; his faithfulness is a shield and buckler.

5 You will not fear the terror of the night, or the arrow that flies by day,

6 or the pestilence that stalks in darkness, or the destruction that wastes at noonday.

7 A thousand may fall at your side, ten thousand at your right hand, but it will not come near you.

8 You will only look with your eyes and see the punishment of the wicked.

9 Because you have made the Lord your refuge,[b] the
Most High your dwelling place, 10 no evil shall befall you,
no scourge comes near your tent.

11 For he will command his angels concerning you to guard you in all your ways.

12 On their hands they will bear you up, so that you will not dash your foot against a stone.

13 You will tread on the lion and the adder, the young lion and the serpent you will trample under foot.

14 Those who love me, I will deliver; I will protect those who know my name.

15 When they call to me, I will answer them; I will be with them in trouble, I will rescue them and honor them.

16 With long life I will satisfy them, and show them my salvation.

Psalm 91

Advice to Ponder

Don't Just

Don't just learn, experience
Don't just read, absorb
Don't just change, transform
Don't just relate, advocate
Don't just promise, prove
Don't just criticize, encourage
Don't just think, ponder
Don't just take, give
Don't just see, feel
Don't just dream, do
Don't just hear, listen
Don't just talk, act
Don't just tell, show
Don't just exist, live

Roy T. Bennett, Author, "The Light in the Heart" (https://www.goodreads.com/quotes/8110791-don-t-just-don-t-just-learn-experience-don-t-just-read-absorb)

Stress Management

In August 2014, I attended a program at North Carolina Central University School of Nursing. This was for a pilot program called ASAP about dealing with stress. Below is a handout from that program. Using this as a guide, think of what you can do to reduce stress in your life.

STRESS MANAGEMENT PROGRAM

ATTITUDE

- Positive thinking
- Refocus the negative to be positive
- Talk positively to yourself
- Plan some fun
- Make an effort to stop negative thoughts

PHYSICAL ACTIVITY

- Start an individualized program of physical fitness
- Decide on a specific time, type, frequency, and level of physical activity

NUTRITION

- Plan to eat foods for improved health and well-being
- Use the food guide pyramid to help select healthy food choices
- Eat an appropriate amount of food on a reasonable schedule

SOCIAL SUPPORT

- Make an effort to interact socially with people
- Reach out to individuals
- Nurture self and others

RELAXATION

- Use relaxation techniques – guided imagery, listening to music, etc.; learn about and try different techniques and choose one or two that work for you
- Take time for personal interests and hobbies
- Listen to your body
- Take a mini retreat

Simple Things That Make a Difference

1. *Eat right – Putting the right things in your body is important. What you put into your body, your vessel, has a direct impact on your total being.*
2. *Drink water*
3. *Exercise to promote your physical well-being*
4. *Treat people the way you'd like to be treated*
5. *Have a personal relationship with God – Proverbs 3:5-6 says "Trust in the Lord with all your heart, and do not rely on your own insight. In all your ways, acknowledge Him, and He will make straight your paths."*
6. *Have empathy for others*
7. *Love well*
8. *Show compassion*
9. *Be loyal and earn loyalty*
10. *Always have an attitude of gratitude*
11. *Practice humility*
12. *Show respect*
13. *Live with integrity*
14. *Maintain your dignity*
15. *Be tenacious with what is important to you*

ZIGLAR'S WHEEL OF LIFE

Zig Ziglar talked about the wheel of life with seven spokes. The sections created by the spokes are **spiritual, financial, physical, intellectual, family, social, and career**. If any spoke is out of alignment, it knocks the others out. If we spend too much time in a certain spoke, our wheel is off balance. However, if we don't spend any time in some areas, our wheel becomes flat. We should take note of areas where we are strong, but really look at the areas where we suffer. The goal is balance. How do you find balance? Here are a few things to consider, and I am sure you can think of more.

1. Regularly reflect and recharge
2. Prioritize
3. Rest
4. Delegate
5. Eliminate
6. Lighten up
7. Work in a work out
8. Add variety for spice and balance to life

A Time for Laughter

Sayings from the Past and Their Meanings

I thought you might enjoy remembering or hearing some sayings from the past. Here are some I remember.

- **Squat that rabbit and hop another**
  — Move on to the next subject
- **Plant you now, dig you later**
  — We've got to go, see you later
- **I was not born yistiddy**
  — Don't try and fool me, not born yesterday
- **Did not just fall off the turnip truck**
  — I know exactly where you are coming from
- **Every tub has to stand on its own bottom**
  — You are responsible for your own actions
- **Keep on trucking**
  — Move out of my way, immediately
- **On your Ps and Qs**
  — On your best behavior
- **Money isn't everything**
  — Important, right next to oxygen

- **For every action, there is a reaction**
  — There are consequences to your actions

- **An object in motion stays in motion**
  — You gotta keep moving

- **An object at rest stays at rest**
  — "No activity" yields dissatisfaction

- **You don't have to eat the whole cow to know it is beef**
  — Just a small piece

- **You reckon**
  — Seriously

- **The pickings are "slim"**
  — Not much to choose from

- **Can't pull the wool over my eyes**
  — Can't very readily fool me

- **Let's get cracking**
  — It's time to go

- **Call it a day**
  — It's quitting time

- **Reach for the stars**
  — The sky is the limit–there are no limitations

- **Say what you mean and mean what you say**
  — Your word is your bond—credibility

- **Come down off that high horse**
  — You're no better than anyone else

- **Some you win, some you lose, some get rained out**
  — Everything we do is not a winner

- **The monkey said when he got his tail cut off, won't be long now…**
  — Time is near

- **Dog stink it**
  — Unbelievable. Oh no…

- **Say it ain't so**
  — You've got to be kidding me

- **What in the world**
  — Really

- **Takes money to make money**
  — You've got to spend to get something

- **Keep it squeaky clean**
  — No vulgar language

- **Good googa-mooga**
  — Horrendous

- **Leave no stone unturned**
  — Check out all possibilities

- **To have a friend, you must be friendly**
  — No arrogance

MATH OF LIFE

ADD *Jesus to your life*

(Romans 10:9-10)

MULTIPLY *your good deeds*

(2 Corinthians 10:8)

DIVIDE *your blessings with others*

(2 Corinthians 9:11)

SUBTRACT *all your fears*

(1 Peter 5:7)

EQUALS *a wonderful life*

(Psalm 16:11)

WORDS TO THE WISE

Personal Planning & Financial Matters

Personal Documents

If you are going to be a winner, it is wise to plan ahead as best you can and as early as you can for financial matters for retirement.

You must be prepared by planning for your personal business. Keep your planning and legal matters up to date not only to assure matters are taken care of as you wish but also to reduce stress and worry on loved ones.

Financial Matters

If your company has a profit-sharing plan matching opportunity or a retirement plan you can contribute to, please take full advantage and put in the maximum allowed. When retirement rolls around, you will be pleasantly surprised. You will receive statements periodically updating you on the funds in your account. While employed, I took sound advice from my older siblings, and not to brag or boast, but because of God's grace coupled with hard work and being with a great company, I retired as a millionaire. Just "do it!" Keep God center and first, stay grounded, and invest in your retirement in the best way you can.

Planning

Keep your personal business in order. Death can come at any time for any color or gender. Plan ahead and put your personal matters in order. Reach out to an attorney or use your bank's attorney to draw up or update as needed these documents:

- General Power of Attorney
- Last Will and Testament
- Living Will and Health Care Power of Attorney
- Designation of a Health Care Agent
- Beneficiary Designations – these will take precedence over your Will
- Update beneficiary designations on life insurance policies and retirement accounts when needed
- Possibly a summary document for your plan

Keep your documents safely and securely stored and retain copies of all documents so that you can access them as needed. Arrange for your Living Will to be sent to your primary care doctors and health care agents.

GRATITUDE

A special thanks to my husband, Lee, my companion, road partner, confidant, and prayer warrior for almost 50 years of friendship, love, and marriage.

My successful career was made less complex and much easier because of your unwavering support. You are a phenomenal father, papa, and a dedicated, hard-working family man. Your most important attributes are that you are God-fearing and you understand the power of prayer.

Words are inadequate to express my sincere gratitude to God for connecting the two of us. What an incredible, exciting, enjoyable journey it has been and still is.

Our love story is yet another chapter . . .

Wedding Day
September 1, 1973

2014

Evelyn &
Lee Booker

2016

If it were not for you,
my wonderful parents,
there would be no me!

ABOUT THE AUTHOR

Evelyn Booker grew up the eighth of ten children in her family. She received her BA in English from North Carolina Central University, married her college sweetheart, and a few years later began an illustrious career with Capitol Broadcasting Company. She was the first African American female to sell television for WRAL-TV in Raleigh, North Carolina. Through her diligence, perseverance, talent, and record-setting work, she moved up the corporate ladder to become General Sales Manager of FOX50-TV, culminating a very successful thirty year career with CBC.

In January 2021, Kevin Hungate of NBCUniversal and one of Evelyn's first hires at WRAZ TV in Raleigh, connected Evelyn to be interviewed by the non-profit advocacy group Black and Brilliant in a partnership event with BOLD at NBCUniversal to create a conversation about mentoring and paying it forward. That conversation can be found at https://sites.google.com/view/theevelynbookerstory/home.

Evelyn is married to Lee Booker. They have two grown daughters and five gifted grandchildren.

Made in the USA
Columbia, SC
20 March 2021

34728056R00085